JESUS OUR GUIDE

JESUS OUR GUIDE

Faith and Life Series

Revised Edition

BOOK FOUR

Ignatius Press, San Francisco
Catholics United for the Faith, Steubenville, Ohio

Nihil Obstat: Rev. James M. Dunfee, S.T.L.
                  Censor Librorum
Imprimatur: + Most Reverend Bishop R. Daniel Conlon
                  Bishop of Steubenville

Director of First Edition: The late Rev. Msgr. Eugene Kevane, Ph.D.
Assistant Director and General Editor of First Edition: Patricia Puccetti Donahoe, M.A.
First Edition Writer: Barbara Nacelewicz
Director and General Editor of Revision: Caroline Avakoff, M.A.
Revision Writer: Colette Ellis, M.A.
Revision Artist: Christopher J. Pelicano

Catholics United for the Faith, Inc., and Ignatius Press gratefully acknowledge the guidance and assistance of the late Reverend Monsignor Eugene Kevane, Director of the Pontifical Catechetical Institute, Diocese of Arlington, Virginia, in the production of the First Edition of this series. The First Edition intended to implement the authentic approach in Catholic catechesis given to the Church through documents of the Holy See and in particular the Conference of Joseph Cardinal Ratzinger on "Sources and Transmission of Faith". The Revised Edition continues this commitment by drawing upon the *Catechism of the Catholic Church* (Libreria Editrice Vaticana, © 1994).

Scripture quotations are from the Holy Bible, Revised Standard Version, Catholic Edition. Old Testament © 1952; Apocrypha © 1957; Catholic Edition, incorporating the Apocrypha, © 1966; New Testament © 1946; Catholic Edition ©1965, by the Division of Christian Education of the National Council of the Churches of Christ in the United States of America. All rights reserved.

The Ad Hoc Committee to Oversee the Use of the Catechism, United States Conference of Catholic Bishops, has found this catechetical text to be in conformity with the *Catechism of the Catholic Church*.

Contents

APPENDIX

A Note to Parents about the Revision

The changes to the fourth grade student text, *Jesus Our Guide*, while minimal, attempt to emphasize the scriptural basis of our Faith in accord with Sacred Tradition. New vocabulary is now indicated by bold type, new words have been introduced to enhance each lesson in the revised text, and each definition can now be found both within the chapter and in the glossary. Common Catholic prayers have been included in an expansive list at the back of the student textbook. In addition, every chapter opens with a Scripture passage, important verses supplement the text where relevant, new questions have been introduced, pre-existing questions have been revised for age-appropriateness, and references to the *Catechism of the Catholic Church* are now specified for each question and answer.

Despite the improvements to the series, it is important to realize that, as parents, you are the primary educators of your children. Your active participation in your child's religious education is highly encouraged. As a family, you are the first witnesses of God's love to your child. If you provide a model of Catholic living at home, if as a family you participate in the sacramental life of the Church, and if you pray and attend Mass together, your children are more likely to take to heart the lessons they learn in religion classes at school. Family discussion of current events with a healthy religious perspective will allow your child to grow up with a better understanding of the world around him, and more importantly, help him to be a Catholic in the midst of it. As stated in the *General Directory for Catechesis*, "family catechesis precedes . . . accompanies and enriches all forms of catechesis" (GDC, 226; Congregation for the Clergy, 1998). Providing your child with a strong Catholic identity at an early age, while not ensuring a lifetime of devotion, will certainly prepare him for the challenges of becoming a faithful Catholic adult.

The *Jesus Our Guide* student text is written on a reading level higher than that of the average fourth grader. This is intentional. It is important for children to hear the Good News in a fuller manner than a more simplified version would allow. Please take the time to review the material with your children, to read the text aloud with them, to study the questions and answers, and to examine and discuss the religious art that accompanies each chapter. By lessening the emphasis on individual student reading, there is more opportunity for your child to concentrate on the Gospel message itself as well as the idea that theology plays an important role in all aspects of his life.

Those who have labored in the revision process of the *Faith and Life* series sincerely hope that it will provide parents, catechists, and teachers with the assistance they need in the task of evangelizing young minds.

INTRODUCTION

Pilgrims to Heaven

> Blessed are the men whose strength is in thee, in whose heart are the highways to Zion.
>
> Psalm 84:5

Has anyone ever called out to you, "Where do you think you're going?" Suddenly you notice you were riding your bicycle right into a main highway. Or has anyone ever asked you, "What do you think you're doing?" as you were lighting some matches?

Sometimes you need to ask yourself, where am I *really* going? What am I *really* doing? You need to know what your goal is: not only your goal for this day, or for tomorrow, or for next year, or for the time you're grown up. You need to know your goal for your whole life and for eternity. That is the most important goal of all, and all your other goals should depend on it.

After you know what your overall goal is, you need to know the directions for getting there. What are you doing? What should you do to get there? If you want to go to your friend's house, you have to know which streets to take and which turns to take. Can you walk there or reach it by bicycle? Or do you have to take a bus, train, or maybe even an airplane? If you have to go to the bus station or airport, you can't just step on to any bus or airplane. You have to know which one leads you to your goal. You have to buy your ticket. You have to know what to do to get on to the right bus or airplane.

You have heard of our pilgrim fathers who first came to America. They were travellers looking for a land of freedom and peace where they could start a new and better life.

You have also heard of pilgrimages. There are pilgrimages to the Holy Land where our Lord lived, to Rome where the Holy Father lives, or to Lourdes or Fatima where our Lady has appeared. A journey to a holy place to worship God is usually called a pilgrimage. We all want to be pilgrims on a great pilgrimage to heaven.

This year you will hear about the pilgrimage of the chosen people of God in the Old Testament, and about Jesus Christ's teachings in the New Testament.

People who travel need a guidebook and a guide. The guidebook for our pilgrimage to heaven is the Bible and our guide is Jesus Christ. He speaks to us through his Church. When the Pope and the bishops teach us something, it is really our guide, Jesus, who is speaking.

This year you will learn what your overall goal in life is. This book will help you learn what to do to get there. This is *by far* the most important thing for you to know.

Q. 1   *What is a pilgrimage?*

A pilgrimage is a journey to a holy place to offer worship to God (CCC 1674).

Q. 2   *How is our life on earth like a pilgrimage?*

Our life on earth is like a pilgrimage because we are here to journey toward our heavenly home, to be united with God and to give him glory and due worship (CCC 302, 853–54).

Q. 3   *What is our guidebook for this pilgrimage?*

The Bible, which is the inspired word of God, is our guidebook for this pilgrimage (CCC 105–108).

Q. 4   *Who is our guide on our pilgrimage to heaven?*

Jesus is our guide on our pilgrimage to heaven (CCC 1698, 2232–33).

Q. 5   *How can we be sure that we are following the guidebook (the Bible) and our guide (Jesus) on our pilgrimage?*

We can be sure that we are following the guidebook, the Bible, and our guide, Jesus, by being faithful to the Church that Jesus founded. Jesus has sent the Holy Spirit to the Church to guard the truths he has given us (CCC 171, 551).

"Thy word is a lamp to my feet and a light to my path."

Psalm 119:105

PART ONE

B.C.
Before Christ

12

CHAPTER 1

The Fall of Man

Then the LORD God said, "Behold, the man has become like one of us, knowing good and evil; and now, lest he put forth his hand and take also of the tree of life, and eat, and live for ever"—therefore the LORD God sent him forth from the garden of Eden, to till the ground from which he was taken.

Genesis 3:22–23

In the Beginning

Before God created the world, he made beautiful creatures called angels. **Angels** are pure spirits created to glorify God and serve him.

All the angels were very good when God created them. But some of them began to think that they were wiser than God. These angels turned against God and wouldn't have anything to do with him. They cut themselves off from him forever. We call the state to which they were condemned hell. Hell is eternal suffering of separation from God.

After God had finished creating the world and all the plants and animals in it, he made a creature in his image. He made a body out of dust from the ground and breathed into its nostrils the breath of life, which was the man's **soul**. The man came to life and God called him **Adam**.

Then God planted a beautiful garden on the earth in a land called **Eden**, and there he placed Adam. A wide river flowed through the garden, making it green and cool. In order to make Adam happy, God also made to grow every tree that was beautiful or had good fruit to eat on it. In the middle of the garden, God placed two special trees. One was the **Tree of Life**. If Adam ate the fruit from this tree, he would be young and strong forever. The other was the **Tree of the Knowledge of Good and Evil**.

When man was created, he was happy. He was never tired or sick. He was surrounded by animals, which he named. But he was lonely. There was no one with whom he could share himself.

"It is not good that the man should be alone. I will make a suitable helpmate for him," said God. So he caused Adam to fall into a deep sleep and took out one of his ribs, which he made into a woman. And then he brought her to Adam.

"At last!" cried Adam. "This is a creature like myself. I will call her woman because she was taken out of man."

Adam and his wife, **Eve**, were very happy in their garden, which was paradise. They were able to walk with God, speak with him, and be very close friends with him. They were completely happy. Their bodies were holy and would not grow old. They would never die. They weren't at all ashamed of being naked. In fact, they never noticed it. They had never even heard of anything bad.

The Test

Adam and Eve loved God. God was the Creator and they were his creatures. He wanted them to love him freely. He wanted to see if they would love and obey him if they had a choice. God gave them a test.

"You may eat the fruit from any tree in the garden," he told them, "except for the Tree of the Knowledge of Good and Evil, which I have put here next to the Tree of Life in the middle of the garden. Do not eat from it. For if you do, you shall die."

The fallen angels in hell hated God. These **devils** were miserable and wanted Adam and Eve to be unhappy too. One day while Adam's wife was walking through the garden, the devil, disguised as a serpent, called to her in a friendly voice, "Won't God let you eat from any of the trees in the garden?"

"Oh no," she answered. "We may eat from all the trees, all but this one in the middle of the garden. God said not even to touch it. If we do, we will die."

"Oh, that's not true. You won't die," lied the devil. "God is afraid that if you eat from that tree, you will become just like him. You will know good and evil."

The woman then saw that the fruit on the tree looked very good. And to think, if only she ate it, she'd be just like God! She picked the fruit and ate it. Then she gave some to Adam and he ate it too.

A Sad Ending

All at once, Adam and Eve felt unhappy because they now knew evil. Before they had known only good; but now they knew what it was like to be bad. Suddenly, they realized they were naked and they were very embarrassed. They looked around and found some leaves from fig trees, which they sewed together to make aprons for themselves.

But even with clothes on, they were miserable and ashamed. Their souls still felt naked because they were wounded, and so they were unhappy. They didn't know quite what to do with themselves. Nothing made them happy or interested them any more. They had sinned.

When it was evening, God came for a walk in the garden. Whereas before Adam and his wife would run to meet and talk with him, now they were so ashamed and afraid that they ran and hid among the trees.

"Adam, where are you?" called God.

Adam answered, "I heard you walking in the garden and I was afraid because I was naked and so I hid from you."

"Who told you that you were naked?" asked God. "Have you eaten from the tree from which I have forbidden you to eat?"

Adam was very ashamed but he had his excuse ready. He wanted God to know that it was not his fault. "The woman that you made for me—she gave me some of the fruit and so I ate it," he said.

Then God asked the woman, "What have you done?"

The woman had someone to blame, too. "The serpent fooled me and so I ate the fruit," she said.

God said to Eve, "I will greatly multiply your pain in childbearing; in pain you shall bring forth children, yet your desire shall be for your husband, and he shall rule over you."

God said to Adam, "Because you have eaten the fruit I forbade you to eat, the ground shall be cursed because of you. You shall have to work hard to get your food from it. It will grow thorns and thistles for you. Only by hard work and sweat will you find food to eat. And this will go on until you, yourself, return to the ground, for now you will die. You were taken from the ground and you will return to it; you are dust and to dust you shall return."

The Promise of a New Beginning

Adam and Eve had lost their Heavenly Father's grace. They could no longer walk and talk with him and be his friends as before. It

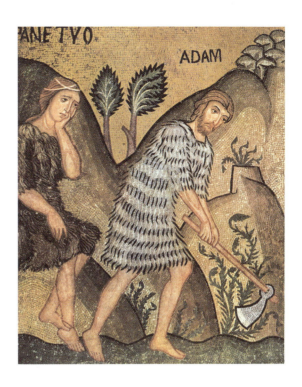

was necessary for them to leave paradise. They would suffer, but in his kindness and love, God still cared for them. He promised that one of their descendants would crush the power of evil that they had brought into the world. One day in the future God would send them a **Redeemer** to save them from sin and open the gates of heaven again. **Heaven** is eternal life and happiness with God.

Out into the world went the poor man and woman, dressed in animal skin clothes that God had made for them. Behind them were angels to guard the entrance to the Garden of Eden so that they could not return.

Adam and Eve settled somewhere outside the Garden of Eden. They must have cleared the land, which had been producing weeds and thorns. They probably gathered wild seeds and sowed them in their newly cleared fields. They may have rounded up enough goats, sheep, and cattle for their needs. They had to work hard.

15

Although they could no longer walk and talk with God, he was watching over them with his loving care. He knew that they were sorry for having offended him.

Adam knew that his wife would have children and that their descendants would fill the whole earth. So he called her "Eve" which means "mother of all the living."

Q. 6 *What is heaven?*

Heaven is eternal life and happiness with God (CCC 1023–24).

Q. 7 *What is hell?*

Hell is the eternal suffering of separation from God (CCC 1033–35).

Q. 8 *What are the angels?*

The angels are pure spirits, created to glorify and serve God (CCC 328–29).

Q. 9 *Was man created weak and sinful as we are now?*

Man was not created weak and sinful as we are now, but was created holy, in a state of happiness (CCC 374–76).

Q. 10 *How is man different from the animals and special in God's eyes?*

Man is different from the animals and special in God's eyes because he possesses an immortal soul (CCC 356–58, 363).

Q. 11 *Why did God test Adam and Eve with the forbidden fruit?*

God tested Adam and Eve with the forbidden fruit in order to give them a chance to obey him freely (CCC 387, 396, 412).

Q. 12 *When Adam and Eve failed God's test, did God abandon them without any hope?*

When Adam and Eve failed God's test, God did not abandon them without any hope. He promised them a Savior and God's final victory over sin and death (CCC 55, 410–11).

CHAPTER 2

The World's First Murder

And the LORD said, "What have you done? The voice of your brother's blood is crying to me from the ground."

Genesis 4:10

Adam and Eve's Children

After a while, Eve gave birth to a child. They named him **Cain**. Then a brother named **Abel** was born. Later, as time went by, Eve would have many more children. These children would have children of their own. Soon there would be many people living on earth.

When Cain and Abel were still young men, Cain became a farmer and Abel became a shepherd. Their father, Adam, must have taught them all about God and how to honor and praise him. They both prepared offerings from their labors to give back to God as a **sacrifice**. In this way, they could show God that they knew that all their blessings had come from him.

Cain brought some crops from his fields and placed them on the stone altar which he had built. On his altar, Abel placed the finest lambs from his flock. Both offerings were set on fire, burned up, and, in this way, sacrificed to God.

The Crime

God was pleased with Abel's sacrifice because he offered his best, which showed that he had faith in his heart. Cain, on the other hand, was envious of Abel and hated him. God saw this hatred in Cain's heart and showed him that he was not happy with Cain's sacrifice. This made Cain furious. He decided to get rid of Abel.

God saw what Cain planned to do and said, "Why are you angry and why do you look so sad? If you do well and try to please me, I will

> *"By faith Abel offered to God a more acceptable sacrifice than Cain, through which he received approval as righteous, God bearing witness by accepting his gifts. . . ."*
>
> *Hebrews 11:4*

accept your sacrifice. Be careful, sin is waiting at your door. You must overcome it."

But the angry man would not listen. "Let us go out into my fields," he said to his brother. Abel loved his brother very much and he did not suspect him. As soon as they were far away from everyone, Cain killed Abel. He left him there, dead and alone, with no one to see what he had done.

The Punishment

Of course, God had seen the terrible thing that Cain had done to his brother. "Where is Abel, your brother?" he asked him.

"I do not know," said Cain. "Am I my brother's keeper?"

"What have you done?" asked God. "Your brother's blood is crying out to me from the ground. Therefore, you will receive your punishment from the ground. From now on, when you try to raise crops, you shall get nothing. And you shall be a wanderer over the whole earth."

Cain pleaded with God, "My punishment is too much to bear. You are driving me away from my farm and I must hide from you. I will be a fugitive on the earth and whoever sees me will kill me!"

God had pity on Cain. "If anyone kills you, I will punish him," he said. And to make sure that no one would harm Cain, God put a mark on him so that people would know to leave him alone. And then Cain went to live in the land of Nod, which was east of Eden. This was the first time God showed that murder was a sin and would be punished.

Another Child

After Cain had gone, Adam and Eve had another son, whom they named **Seth**. "God has given me another child to replace Abel, who was killed by Cain," Eve said.

Eventually, both Seth and Cain married and had children of their own. It was from Seth's descendants that Jesus came. He was the one promised by God to Adam and Eve who would conquer the power of evil.

> "If you are offering your gift at the altar, and there remember that your brother has something against you, leave your gift there before the altar and go; first be reconciled to your brother, and then come and offer your gift."
>
> Matthew 5:23–24

Words to Know:

Cain   Abel   sacrifice   Seth

Q. 13   *Is murder wrong in God's eyes?*

Yes, murder is very wrong in God's eyes, and it is forbidden by the Fifth Commandment (CCC 2268).

Q. 14   *Why was Abel's sacrifice acceptable, while Cain's was not?*

Abel's sacrifice was offered with faith and love, and so his sacrifice was pleasing to God, while Cain's sacrifice was not (Heb 11:4).

Q. 15   *Did God stop loving Cain because of his sin?*

No, God did not stop loving Cain because of his sin. God marked Cain to protect him and sent him away to do penance (CCC 1856, 1430, Gen 4:11–16).

CHAPTER 3

Turning Away from God

For behold, I will bring a flood of waters upon the earth, to destroy all flesh in which is the breath of life from under heaven; everything that is on the earth shall die. But I will establish my covenant with you; and you shall come into the ark, you, your sons, your wife, and your sons' wives with you.

Genesis 6:17–18

The Flood

Many years went by after Seth, Cain, and the other children of Adam and Eve had settled in several parts of the world. Gradually, even the descendants of Seth began to forget about God and to think only about the pleasures of this

life. They started to do bad things to get what they wanted. God saw that they were constantly thinking and planning evil things. And he was sorry that he had made them. Patiently, he waited, giving them many chances to change their ways and to turn to him again. But their crimes only grew worse.

Noah, who was one of the descendants of Seth, was the only man on earth who tried to please God. God decided that he would wash all that was evil from the earth and begin again with Noah and his family.

So one day God called, "Noah, the earth is filled with violence. I am going to wash it clean with a flood. Make yourself a boat out of wood and cover it inside and out with pitch to make it watertight. When it is finished you, your wife, your sons, and their wives are to go inside. Take on board a male and female of every kind of animal. You may take seven pairs of the animals that you are used to eating. Finally, fill the hold of the ship with other food for yourselves and for the animals."

"By faith Noah, warned about things not yet seen, revered God and built an ark that his household might be saved. He therefore condemned the world and inherited the justice which comes through faith."

Hebrews 11:7

Noah and his sons—**Shem**, **Japheth**, and **Ham**—set to work to build the **ark**, which is another name for the boat. At last, everything was ready. All the animals were herded inside, two of every kind of creeping thing and of every kind of bird. After all the animals were in, Noah and his family entered the ark and closed the door.

Soon a heavy rain began to pour from the skies and continued for forty days and forty nights. As the waters rose above the highest mountains, the ark was gently lifted up and carried along on the enormous sea that God had made with the rain. But inside, the family was safe and dry.

A New Beginning

The ark floated on for more than a month and Noah's family inside began to grow restless and to long for firm ground. Eventually, God sent a strong wind to blow over the earth and push back the waters. Finally, the ark came to rest on the top of a mountain known as Ararat; just the tip of the mountain was above water. But Noah could not tell just how far the water had gone down. So he took one of the doves from the ark and let her fly off to look for land. But the dove found no place to settle and returned to Noah. He waited seven days and then again sent forth the dove and it returned before evening. This time it carried in its beak a freshly plucked branch from an olive tree. Then Noah knew that the waters were

nearly gone from the earth. He waited another seven days and once more sent out the dove. It did not return to them but settled down in the newly dried land. That was the sign Noah had been waiting for. He threw open the big door that had been bolted for so long and looked out. The ground was dry!

God called to him, "Come forth out of the ark. And let the animals go so that they can have young and once again there will be many of them on earth."

So at long last, everyone came out of the ark. The very first thing that Noah did was build an altar to offer the best of his animals to God in thanksgiving for having brought them safely to land again. God was very pleased with Noah's sacrifice and said to himself, "I

will never again destroy every living creature on the earth."

God said to Noah and his sons, "Have many children and fill the earth. I am making a covenant with you and your descendants. Never again will a flood come to destroy the entire earth. As a sign of this **covenant**, I have put a rainbow in the sky. Whenever a rainbow appears, I will remember my promise that never again will I allow a flood to destroy the earth."

So Noah and his sons and their wives settled on the land and began to work the earth which had been covered by water for so long. They dug it up and planted seeds. Noah's three sons eventually moved to various parts of the world and had large families. Of the three, Shem was the most blessed by God. Jesus, the Savior of the world promised to Adam and Eve, came

from Shem's family. And Japheth was also blessed. But Ham wasn't a good man. His son, **Canaan**, settled in a beautiful and fertile land, which was named after him, but his descendants grew so wicked that God took the land of Canaan away from them and gave it to the descendants of Shem.

The Tower of Babel

Some of the descendants of Shem migrated from the east to the land of Shinar. These people grew very proud of all their abilities. They forgot that these talents had really come from God. Once more God was disappointed in men. After they had built a fine city for themselves, they remarked, "Look how wonderful we are. We did this all by ourselves. We can do anything we want. Next we'll build a tower with its top in the heavens. Then we'll really make a name for ourselves!"

So they set to work on their tower using bricks made of clay and held together with tar. Higher and higher up went the tower.

But God wasn't pleased with their proud hearts. More and more they would think it was all their own doing and forget how much they needed God's help. So God confused their language so that they could not understand one another. They had to give up building the tower because they could no longer work together.

There was such a babble of shouting and confusion as each person tried to make himself understood that their tower came to be known as the **Tower of Babel**. Eventually the people living in the city drifted away to different parts of the earth, leaving their tower unfinished.

In this way God showed men that it is a grave sin to turn away from him.

Words to Know:

Noah   Shem   Japheth   Ham   ark
     covenant   Canaan   Tower of Babel

Q. 16   *Why did God send the flood?*

God sent the flood to wash away evil from the earth and save the human race (CCC 56, 71).

Q. 17   *How do we know from the story of Noah that the human family is very important to God?*

We know that the human family is very important to God because God saved Noah, his wife, his three sons, and their wives on the ark during the great flood (CCC 56, 58, 2203, Gen 6:18).

Q. 18   *Did God want division among the nations?*

No, division among the nations was the result of the sin of pride committed at Babel (CCC 57).

"When pride comes, then comes disgrace, but with the humble is wisdom."

Proverbs 11:2

CHAPTER 4

God Prepares a People For the Savior

"By myself I have sworn, says the LORD, because you have done this, and have not withheld your son, your only son, I will indeed bless you, and I will multiply your descendants as the stars of heaven and as the sand which is on the seashore. And your descendants shall possess the gate of their enemies, and by your descendants shall all the nations of the earth bless themselves, because you have obeyed my voice."

Genesis 22:16–18

Abram

Among the descendants of Shem was a man named Abram. God had something special in mind for Abram. One day God called to him, "Abram, leave your country, your house, and all your relatives, and come away to a land that I will show you and I will make you a great nation. I will bless you and make your name great."

To leave his home, to leave his relatives and friends, to wander the earth until God would tell him to stop? How could God make a great nation out of someone who roamed the desert with no real home? But Abram had always loved God, and he believed that God was telling him the truth.

And so Abram, his wife, Sarai, and his nephew, Lot, packed up their tents, gathered together their herds of cattle. Along with a few relatives and some servants, set forth on their pilgrimage to a strange land. Although the fam-

ily suffered in strange lands from famine and other hardships, Abram remained obedient to the Lord. He even built an altar on a mountaintop to call on the name of the Lord.

During that time, Abram waited patiently for God to show him where to stop. He trusted the Lord.

One day they arrived in a beautiful land—green hills covered with wildflowers. There were trees heavy with ripe olives. Bordering the land was a sparkling blue-green sea—the sea which today is known as the Mediterranean. The land itself was called Canaan. Abram and his family settled on this land.

(Lot had settled in the Jordan plain, in the cities of Sodom and Gomorrah. Later on the people in these two cities were so wicked and depraved that God rained brimstone and fire on them. The cities were utterly destroyed. But Lot, a just man, was saved.)

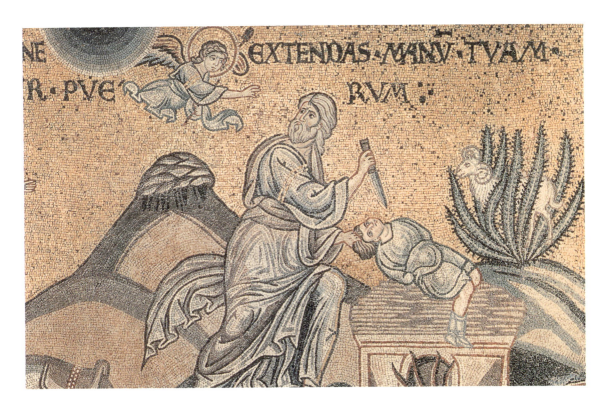

One day God said to Abram, "Lift up your eyes and look north, south, east, and west. Everything that you see I will give to you and your descendants forever. They will be as many as the grains of sand on the earth."

As time went on Abram did many good things which pleased God very much. Once, Abram's nephew, Lot, was taken prisoner when Sodom, the city he lived in, was attacked by invading armies. Abram got together all his servants and shepherds. They defeated the enemy and caused them to run away. He rescued his kinsman and allies. Although the kings of those neighboring cities wanted to reward Abram, he refused, for he knew that his reward would come from God. But one of the kings, Melchizedek, king of Salem, brought bread and wine as a gift. He was also a priest of God and he blessed Abram. And Abram had a vision in which God spoke to him and said: "Fear not, Abram, I am your shield. Your reward shall be very great."

Then the sorrow that had been weighing upon Abram's soul burst out at last. God had promised him and Sarai many descendants but they were both old and childless. "O Lord God!" he cried out. "What could you give me? Of what use is all I possess? You haven't given me any children. In fact, when I die, everything will go to my chief servant, Eleazer."

Then God answered, "Your own son shall be your heir and not Eleazer. Look up to the heavens and count all the stars if you can. Your descendants will be as many as the stars!" Although he was a very old man, had no children, and Sarai was beyond childbearing age, Abram believed God.

The Covenant

One day, God appeared to Abram and said, "I am God Almighty. Walk before me and be blameless and I will make my covenant between me and you and your descendants forever. I will give your descendants this land of Canaan and I will be their God." Abram fell on his face in fear and wonder. And God said, "You shall be the father of many nations. No longer shall your name be Abram, but you shall be called **Abraham**, which means 'father of many people'." God gave Sarai a new name, too. Her name would be **Sarah**, which means "princess."

Every covenant or contract has two parts. For his part, God would watch over Abraham's descendants in a special way and give them the land of Canaan. For their part, these special people chosen by God would keep themselves apart from others and do special things as a sign that they were dedicated to God. In this way, God was preparing them for the birth of Jesus, who would come from this people.

One Final Test

Just as God had promised, Abraham and Sarah *did* have a son and they named him **Isaac**. They were delighted with their child who was born to them in their old age. But God wanted to test Abraham's faith. One day he said, "Abraham, take your only son Isaac, whom you love, up to the mountains and sacrifice him to me as a burnt offering."

What was this? Abraham's own dear son, Isaac, for whom he had waited so long, to be put on an altar, killed, and offered to God! God was taking back the wonderful gift that he had given.

But Abraham didn't complain, and he wasn't angry with God. He believed that God would work things out for the best. Hadn't God promised that Isaac would be his heir? God could do anything and he wasn't cruel and heartless—Abraham knew that. Abraham had to believe and obey.

A Happy Ending

Abraham rose early the next morning and loaded his donkey with firewood, food, and water. Two of his servants stood ready to accompany him. "Come, Isaac," he said to his son. "We are going to the mountains in Moriah."

They walked for three days, but finally Abraham saw the mountain. "Stay here with the donkey," he said to his servants. "The boy and I will climb this mountain and worship God."

So they went up together. Isaac looked at his father in wonder. "Father," he asked, "we have fire and wood, but where is the lamb for the sacrifice?"

"God himself will provide the lamb for the sacrifice, my son," Abraham replied.

When they reached the top, Abraham set about building an altar. He piled up the wood and then tied Isaac's hands and feet and placed him on the altar. And then Abraham picked up the knife to slay his son. Suddenly an angel of the Lord called to him from heaven and said, "Abraham, Abraham!" and he answered, "Here I am." The angel said, "Do not touch the boy or

Father, . . . look with favor on these offerings and accept them as once you accepted the gifts of your servant Abel, the sacrifice of Abraham, our father in faith, and the bread and wine offered by your priest Melchizedek.

First Eucharistic Prayer of the Mass

> Now the promises were made to Abraham and to his offspring. It does not say, "And to offsprings," referring to many; but referring to one, "And to your offspring," which is Christ.
>
> Galatians 3:16

do anything to him, for now I know that you love and fear God because you were willing to give up your only son."

Abraham untied Isaac. At that moment, he saw a wild ram caught by its horns in a bush. They took the ram and offered it as a sacrifice in the place of Isaac. Abraham had believed God and God *had* provided for him.

All through his life Abraham trusted the Lord, in spite of the fact that many times it seemed impossible to trust and believe. All the odds seemed against him. God tested the faith of Abraham because he wanted to make him the father of a holy people. God rewarded his humble submission and obedience. That is why even to this day we call Abraham, "our father in faith."

Words to Know:

Abraham   Sarah   Isaac

Q. 19   *Why is Abraham called our father in faith?*
Abraham is called our father in faith because God made him the father of a holy people (CCC 59 [Gen 22:12], CCC 144–47).

Q. 20   *Why did God test Abraham?*
God tested Abraham to allow him to choose to be faithful to God (Gen 22:12).

Q. 21   *How did God bless Abraham for passing his test?*
God blessed Abraham for passing his test by giving him many descendants, who would also share in Abraham's blessing. God would also bless Abraham's descendants by giving them the land of their enemies (CCC 60, Gen 22:15–18).

CHAPTER 5

The People of Israel

And God said to him, "Your name is Jacob; no longer shall your name be called Jacob, but Israel shall be your name." So his name was called Israel. And God said to him, "I am God Almighty: be fruitful and multiply; a nation and a company of nations shall come from you, and kings shall spring from you. The land which I gave to Abraham and Isaac I will give to you, and I will give the land to your descendants after you."

Genesis 35:10–12

The Birthright

When Isaac became a man, Abraham sent a servant back to the country of his birth to find a wife for Isaac among his relatives. Abraham didn't want him to marry a Canaanite woman. One day the servant returned with a lovely girl named **Rebekah**. She and Isaac fell in love at first sight and were soon married.

For a long time, Isaac asked God for children. God finally granted his prayer: Rebekah gave birth to twins, whom she named **Jacob** and **Esau**.

As the boys grew up, Esau turned out to be a rough mountain man. He was strong and loved to hunt with his bow and arrow and slingshot. Esau was Isaac's favorite. Jacob, on the other hand, was his mother's favorite.

Because Esau was the first of the twins to be born, he was considered the eldest son. Usually the eldest son had a right to be head of the family after the father died. This right was called a "birthright." However, the Lord had told

Rebekah, while the twins were still in her womb, that the elder was to serve the younger.

Once, when Jacob was cooking some pottage, a kind of vegetable stew, by his tent. Esau, who had been out hunting all day, came home very hungry. How good the stew smelled! "Give me some of your stew. I'm starving!" Esau demanded.

Jacob then said, "I will give you some on the condition that you give me your birthright in exchange."

"What good is my birthright to me anyway when I'm about to starve to death?" said Esau.

"Swear first," insisted Jacob.

So Esau swore before God that he would give his place as eldest son to Jacob. Jacob gave him a large bowl of stew, some bread, and a cup of wine. Esau ate and drank, and went his way. By this, he showed how little he cared for his birthright.

The Blessing

When Isaac grew old and nearly blind, he called Esau one day and said to him, "My son, I'm very old and will probably die soon. Since you are my eldest son, I want to give you my blessing. But I'm too weak. Take your bow and arrow and hunt some game and make me some spicy meat, as you know I like, so that I may eat and have enough strength to bless you."

So Esau went on his errand. As soon as he was out of sight, Rebekah, who had heard this, ran to find Jacob. She told him what Isaac had said to Esau and then said, "I have a plan for you to get the blessing instead of Esau. Kill two fat and tender kid goats, and I will cook them with spices he likes, so that when he has eaten, he may bless you before he dies."

"But Esau is so rough and hairy and I am not. If my father touches me, he will find out that I am Jacob and then he will curse instead of bless me," argued Jacob.

But Rebekah replied that he should do as she asked and she would take the responsibility.

As soon as the food was prepared, Rebekah gave Jacob Esau's best clothes to put on. Then she took the skins of the two goats and sewed them on his hands and around his neck. And Jacob brought him the meat and bread. "Father," he called.

"Who is it?" asked Isaac, who was nearly blind.

"I am Esau. Here is the food you asked for. Eat of it, and then you can bless me."

"How did you find the game so quickly, my son?"

"God led me to it."

"You sound so much like Jacob. Come closer to help me know if you are really Esau." So Jacob went and sat down on the side of his father's bed. Isaac clasped his hand. "The voice is indeed the voice of Jacob; but the hands are the hands of Esau. Are you really Esau?"

"I am."

So Isaac ate the meat prepared by Rebekah and drank some wine. After this he said, "Come and kiss me, my son." So Jacob kissed him. Isaac smelled Esau's clothes, and then he gave Jacob his blessing.

> "See, the smell of my son
>   is as the smell of a field which the
>   LORD has blessed!
> May God give you of the dew of heaven,
>   and of the fatness of the earth,
>   and plenty of grain and wine.
> Let peoples serve you,
>   and nations bow down to you.
> Be lord over your brothers,
>   and may your mother's sons bow
>   down to you.
> Cursed be every one who curses you,
> and blessed be every one who blesses
>   you!"

Isaac's blessing of Jacob,
Genesis 27:27–29

29

Jacob was no sooner gone than Esau came in from his hunting. He prepared the food quickly and ran to his father's tent. "Arise, my father, and eat the meat, and then bless me," he said.

"Who is it?" asked Isaac, puzzled.

"I am your first-born son, Esau."

Isaac's voice was trembling and his hands were shaking. "Who just brought me some spicy meat? I ate it, and then I blessed him. My blessing can't be changed."

Esau cried out loudly and bitterly, "Father, bless me too!"

"Your brother, Jacob, must have tricked me and he has taken away your blessing." So he gave Esau a lesser blessing.

Esau remembered how Jacob had also gotten his birthright. "This is the second time that he has tricked me!" he cried. "First my birthright and now my blessing!" He was so angry that he decided to kill Jacob, but Rebekah found out and sent Jacob to live with her brother, Laban, in far away Haran.

Wives for Jacob

Jacob's uncle Laban had two daughters, **Leah** and **Rachel**. Jacob fell in love with Rachel, the younger one, and asked for permission to marry her. Laban answered that if Jacob worked for him for seven years, then he could marry Rachel as a reward.

Jacob gladly agreed—nothing would be too difficult in order to win the beautiful Rachel. Finally the seven years were over and the day of the wedding came. The bride had a veil over her face. But once they were married, Jacob received a big surprise. Laban had tricked him— Jacob had married Leah instead! Laban told him that it was the custom to give the older daughter in marriage first. But he said to Jacob, "If you serve me for another seven years, you can marry Rachel as well." So Jacob worked

for Laban for seven more years and then married Rachel.

Leah knew that Jacob really loved Rachel. But God loved Leah and consoled her. He sent her many children but he sent none to Rachel. One of Leah's sons was named **Judah**. It was from him that Jesus, the Savior of the world, would be descended.

Rachel was very envious of Leah because she had so many children. However, after many years, God sent her a child, whom she named Joseph. Later she had another child, whom she called Benjamin.

A New Name

One day, God told Jacob that it was time for him to take his family and move back to Canaan. And so the family journeyed back to the Promised Land.

Esau was a rough and quick-tempered man. He did things too quickly, without thinking about the consequences, but he had a generous and forgiving heart. He had long since forgiven Jacob and now he was so happy to see his brother return home that he cried with joy.

Once Jacob was settled again in Canaan, God appeared to him and said, "I am God Almighty. You shall no longer be called Jacob but **Israel**. This land which I gave to Abraham and Isaac I will give to you and your descendants after you."

And so Jacob was called Israel. His twelve sons had many children and they became a great nation. They were often called the chil-

For there the LORD has commanded the blessing, life for evermore.

Psalm 133:3

30

dren or the **people of Israel**. Sometimes, they were also called **Hebrews** from Eber, who was a descendant of Shem and a forefather of Abraham. Later, they were called **Jews**, from the name of Judah, who was one of the sons of Jacob and Leah. This is the name by which we know the people of Israel today.

Words to Know:

Rebekah   Jacob   Esau
Leah   Rachel   Judah
Israel   people of Israel
Hebrews   Jews

Q. 22   *Why did Rebekah want Jacob to receive Abraham's blessing instead of Esau?*

Rebekah wanted Jacob to receive Abraham's blessing instead of Esau because she favored Jacob and because God had told her, "the elder shall serve the younger" (Gen 25:23).

Q. 23   *How did God show Jacob that it was wrong to trick people?*

God showed Jacob that it was wrong to trick people by letting Laban trick Jacob into marrying Leah instead of Rachel, the one whom Jacob really loved (Gen 29:25).

Q. 24   *From where did the name of Israel come?*

The name Israel was given by God to Jacob, when Jacob returned to Canaan. This name was passed on to his descendants (Gen 35:10–12).

CHAPTER 6

Joseph Goes to Egypt

The LORD was with Joseph, and he became a successful man; and he was in the house of his master the Egyptian.

Genesis 39:2

The Brothers' Hatred

Eventually Israel (Jacob) grew to be an old man. He was very proud of all twelve of his sons but he particularly loved **Joseph**. He made him a beautiful, long robe out of fine cloth. When the brothers saw that Israel favored Joseph, they were full of envy. They began to hate him and could not even say a kind word to him.

What made it worse was that Joseph started having unusual dreams. One morning, he said, "I dreamed we were harvesting wheat. As we made bundles out of the wheat, my bundle stood up and your bundles all gathered around mine and bowed down to it."

His brothers answered, "Do you think we're ever going to bow down to *you*?"

And then Joseph had another dream where even his father thought he had gone too far. "The sun, the moon, and eleven stars were bowing down to me."

His father scolded him, "What do you mean? Shall I, your mother, and your eleven brothers bow down before you?" And the brothers hated him all the more, but Israel thought these things over and wondered. Perhaps God was speaking to Joseph.

Once, when the brothers were out in the fields with their sheep and were a long way from home, Israel grew anxious about them. "Joseph, go and see how your brothers are and then come and tell me."

Joseph went on his way, wearing his bright coat. After three days' journey, he finally saw them a long way off in their pasturing grounds. But the brothers had seen him too. "Here comes the little dreamer. Let's kill him and throw his body into a well. We can tell our father that a wild animal ate him. That will put an end to his dreams," they said.

The oldest brother, Reuben, wanted to save Joseph and came up with a plan. "Do not take his life or shed his blood, but throw him into this dry well," he said. (He planned to return later and pull Joseph out.) And so the brothers rushed at Joseph and tore off his fine coat and then they threw him in the well.

Afterward, as they were eating their bread, they looked up and saw a caravan of merchants on their way to Egypt, their camels loaded with gum, balm, and myrrh. That gave Judah an idea. "Instead of leaving Joseph in the well to die, let us sell him as a slave to those merchants. After

33

all, he is our brother and so we shouldn't kill him," he said.

So they struck a bargain with the traders and sold him for twenty pieces of silver. Then, when Joseph was on his way to Egypt, the brothers returned to their father with Joseph's coat, which they had dipped in the blood of a goat. They told Israel that Joseph had been killed by a wild animal. Poor Israel nearly died with sorrow, for he had loved Joseph so very much.

God Protects His Child

Meanwhile, God was taking care of Joseph. Upon arriving in Egypt, the merchants sold him to a rich man. And Joseph was put in charge of running the man's house. He did it so well that he was given a lot of money and many privileges. Unfortunately, he was accused of a crime he didn't commit and was thrown in prison. But God was with Joseph, even in prison, and he was soon put in charge of the other prisoners.

One day, the supreme ruler of Egypt, who was called the **Pharaoh**, was displeased with two of his servants, his baker and his butler. He had them thrown into jail. That night they both had unusual dreams. With God's help, Joseph told them what their dreams meant. He said that the butler would work for the Pharaoh again and that the baker would be hanged. And things happened just as he had predicted. The butler, who got out of prison, forgot all about Joseph for two years.

The Great Famine

Then one night Pharaoh had a bad dream. The next morning he called together all his magicians and wise men, but none knew what the dream meant. All of a sudden, the butler remembered Joseph and told Pharaoh about his and the baker's dreams in prison. Joseph was sent for. "Tell me your dream, Pharaoh, and God will reveal what it means," he said.

"In my dream," began Pharaoh, "I was standing on the bank of the Nile River when seven beautiful, fat cows came down to the edge to feed and drink. Just then, seven thin, ugly cows came up behind the fat cows and ate them up, but after they had eaten, they were just as thin as before!"

"God is letting you know what is about to happen," said Joseph. "The seven fat and healthy cows mean that for seven years there will be good crops and plenty of food in Egypt. But the seven thin cows stand for seven years of famine to follow when the rains won't come and the crops won't grow. What you should do is save up some of the food from the good days so that there will be enough food for everyone once the famine begins."

Pharaoh was so impressed with Joseph and his advice that he put him in charge of this project. He made Joseph governor of Egypt, almost as powerful as himself. He gave him gold, fine clothes, and his second best chariot. He also ordered the whole kingdom to bow down to Joseph when he went by.

Joseph set to work during the seven years of plenty to store up enough for the next seven years. Finally, the seven good years came to an end. The Nile River dried up and was little more than a trickle; crops stopped growing. Everywhere people were starting to get very hungry. But Joseph was ready: he opened up the storehouses and began to sell grain and other food to the Egyptians.

Through these events and the ones in the next chapter, we see how God can always bring good out of evil. He always has loving plans for the salvation of his people. Through the sufferings of Joseph, the Jewish people will be protected from famine and will be saved.

Words to Know:

Joseph   Pharaoh

Q. 25 *How did God communicate with Joseph?*
God communicated with Joseph through his dreams (Gen 37:5–11).

Q. 26 *Why did God allow Joseph to be sold into slavery in Egypt?*
God allowed Joseph to be sold into slavery in Egypt to save his people from the great famine (Gen 45:5–11).

"So it was not you who sent me here, but God; and he has made me a father to Pharaoh, and lord of all his house and ruler over all the land of Egypt."

Genesis 45:8

36

CHAPTER 7

The People of Israel Go to Egypt

And he said, "Behold, I have heard that there is grain in Egypt; go down and buy grain for us there, that we may live, and not die."

Genesis 42:2

The Brothers Go to Egypt

The Land of Canaan was also suffering from the famine. So when Israel heard about the food in Egypt, he sent his sons to buy some. But he kept little Benjamin with him because he was afraid that he would lose him as he had lost Joseph.

In Egypt, the ten brothers bowed down with their faces to the ground before the great lord, governor of the land. Joseph remembered his dream. He had recognized them at once but he treated them like strangers and spoke roughly to them. "Where do you come from?" he demanded.

"From Canaan," they replied.

"You are spies," said Joseph, pretending that he did not know who they were.

"Oh no, we're honest men, all brothers. We have come to buy food since there is none in our land."

"I'm sure you must be spies," insisted Joseph.

"No, we are twelve brothers. One is dead and the youngest is at home with our father."

"I still think you are spies and I should kill you, but I will give you a chance to prove that you are not. I will keep one of you in prison to make sure you come back. The rest, go home and bring me your youngest brother so that I will know if you are telling the truth." And he gave orders to have their bags filled with grain and food.

The brothers started talking together in the Hebrew language, not realizing that Joseph could understand. "It's all our fault for having sold Joseph. He cried out for us to save him and we wouldn't listen. Now we are punished for our sin." Joseph was so touched when he saw that his brothers were sorry that he had to leave the room because he was crying.

So they left their brother, Simeon, in jail and went home. They told their father, Israel, about the bargain they had made with the great lord in

Egypt—that they must bring back Benjamin if they wanted Simeon to be released and if they wanted to buy more grain.

The Brothers Return with Benjamin

At first, Israel could not bear to part with Benjamin. But when the food was all gone, he gave in. The nine brothers returned to Egypt with little Benjamin and also some presents from Israel to the great Egyptian lord.

Once again, they stood before Joseph. When Joseph saw that they had brought Benjamin, he told his steward to prepare a feast because he wanted to dine with them. As Joseph came in for dinner, the brothers all bowed down low before him. "How are you?" he asked. "Is your father still alive? Is he well?"

Joseph looked at his little brother, Benjamin, and was so happy to see him that he felt tears coming to his eyes. He went off into a room by himself and wept. Finally, he washed his face and returned to the brothers. "Let food be served," he commanded the steward.

Joseph gave his brothers much delicious food, but to Benjamin he gave more than to anyone else. They all ate and drank and were very happy.

The Secret Comes Out

At last the brothers were ready to depart for home. Each had a sack full of grain, but Joseph put his own silver cup into Benjamin's sack.

Then, as soon as they were gone, Joseph sent his steward after them. "My master thinks that you have stolen his silver cup," he said.

"No we did not," they protested. "Search us if you want. We are honest men. If one of us has taken it, we will be your master's slaves."

The poor brothers were surprised and terrified to see the steward pull the cup out of Benjamin's sack. The steward led them back to Egypt. "Did you think that you could get away with this crime?" demanded Joseph.

"We'll be your slaves," they replied.

"No, I will be merciful. I will take the one who had the cup for my slave. The rest of you can go free."

Judah came forward and fell on his knees. "Please," he begged, "take me for your slave instead of Benjamin. Our father will surely die if he doesn't return home."

Joseph could pretend no longer. Quickly, he ordered everyone but the brothers to leave the room. When he was alone with them, he began to cry so loudly that everyone in the palace heard him. "I am Joseph, your brother," he said. "Is my father really still alive?" The brothers just stared first in disbelief and then in guilt. "I really *am* Joseph, whom you sold as a slave. But do not be angry with yourselves, because God sent me before you. It was part of his plan to save you, his chosen people, from starvation. I needed to come to Egypt so that I could store up food for the famine. If I had not come here no one would have known to expect the famine and you would have died. Now God has made

"Thus says your son Joseph, God has made me lord of all Egypt; come down to me, do not tarry; you shall dwell in the land of Goshen, and you shall be near me, you and your children and your children's children, and your flocks, your herds, and all that you have."

Genesis 45:9–10

me a close friend of Pharaoh and the governor of Egypt. Please go home and bring our father back to live in Egypt. You can have the land of Gesen for your own."

Then he fell upon his brother Benjamin's neck and wept, and he kissed all his brothers. He then gave them wagons filled with provisions and gifts. They went back to Canaan and told the whole story to their father. Israel wasn't sure if he should leave the Promised Land of Canaan to go to Egypt. But one night, in a vision, God spoke to him. "I am God, the God of your father Isaac. Do not be afraid to go to Egypt. Your descendants will be there for a long time, but I will bring them back into Canaan."

At last, after a long journey, father and son were reunited. The father said to Joseph, "Now I shall die with joy because I have at last seen your face, and you are alive." Israel (Jacob) eventually died in Egypt. Joseph took his body back to Canaan and buried him beside Abraham, Isaac, Rebekah, and Leah.

Q. 27 *Why did the people of Israel come to live in Egypt?*

The people of Israel came to live in Egypt because of the rule and authority of Joseph. Pharaoh gave them the best land because he loved Joseph dearly (Gen 45:9–10, 18).

Q. 28 *Were the people of Israel to stay in Egypt?*

No, the people of Israel were not to stay in Egypt. They went there for safety and food during the famine, but it was God's plan to bring them back to the Promised Land (Gen 46:3–4).

"Judah is a lion's whelp; . . . The scepter shall not depart from Judah . . . until he comes to whom it belongs."

Genesis 49:9—10

CHAPTER 8

God's People Suffer in Egypt

"Come, I will send you to Pharaoh that you may bring forth my people, the sons of Israel, out of Egypt."

Exodus 3:10

Slavery in Egypt

The twelve sons of Israel (Jacob) eventually died in Egypt and left behind many children. Except for Joseph's, each son's descendants came to be known as his **tribe**. These tribes lived in Egypt for a long time. Many pharaohs had come and gone since the time of Joseph's friend and now there was one who didn't like the children of Israel. They did not worship the many Egyptian gods. Also, this pharaoh thought that, if Egypt should ever be attacked, the Israelites might side with the enemy.

Pharaoh decided to make slaves of the people of Israel. In this way they would not be able to rebel against their masters. They would die early, worn out from building great pyramids and other buildings and whole cities.

But after the Israelites (also known as Hebrews) became slaves, Pharaoh was still worried. So he thought of another plan, worse than the first: every son born to the Hebrews was to be thrown into the Nile River. The Hebrews tried to hide their newborn sons, but the babies were almost always discovered and snatched away from them.

Moses

Then, one day, a little boy was born into the tribe of Levi. (This tribe or family was descended from Levi, one of the sons of Israel.) When his mother and sister couldn't hide him any longer, they put him in a basket covered with pitch and tar (to make it watertight) and set him afloat in the reeds that grew in the waters along the banks of the Nile.

The mother went home, but his sister, Miriam, hid in the reeds to see what would happen to her little brother. Soon a princess, one of the Pharaoh's daughters, came down to the Nile to bathe. She saw the basket among the reeds, so she sent her maid to get it. When it was opened, they found a baby boy, crying. The

Pharaoh's daughter took pity on him and said, "This must be a Hebrew child."

Miriam came up and asked, "Shall I get a Hebrew woman to nurse the child for you?"

"Yes, please do," answered the princess. Then Miriam brought her mother, the baby's own mother.

"Woman, take this child and nurse him; I will pay you," said the princess.

When the child grew up, his real mother brought him to the palace to Pharaoh's daughter. The princess treated him like a son, and named him "**Moses**," which means that he was saved from the water. Moses grew up in the Pharaoh's palace. He knew that he was a Jew— a descendant of Abraham. He learned about the God of Abraham, Isaac, and Jacob, and he also knew of the great sufferings of his people.

One day, Moses saw an Egyptian beating a Hebrew slave, and in his anger, he ran up and killed the Egyptian when no one was watching. Quickly, he buried the man in the sand. However, someone found out about it.

When Pharaoh heard of it, he wanted Moses killed. But Moses escaped from Egypt to the land of Midian and there he became a shepherd for a man named Jethro.

God Raises Up
A Great Prophet

Meanwhile, God's people in Egypt were bitterly oppressed. They were suffering more and more and were calling out to God to save them. God heard their cries and remembered the covenant he had made with Abraham, Isaac, and Jacob. Now God was ready to begin rescuing his people.

One day, while Moses was guarding his flock he came to Horeb, the mountain of God. There he saw a bush burning. As he came closer, he noticed that the fire was not hurting the bush. An angel of the Lord appeared in the flame. Then God called to him out of the fiery bush. "Moses! Moses!"

"Here I am," answered Moses.

"Do not come any nearer. Take off your shoes, for the place on which you stand is holy ground. I am the God of your father, the God of Abraham, the God of Isaac, and the God of Jacob." And Moses hid his face because he was afraid to look at God. "I have seen how much my people suffer in Egypt. I have heard their cries. I have seen their oppression. I have come to deliver them. I will bring them out of Egypt to return to Canaan, a land that is flowing with milk and honey. And I will send you to Pharaoh that you may bring forth my people out of Egypt."

"But if I go to the children of Israel and say that the God of their fathers has sent me to save them, they will ask what his name is. What shall I say?"

God replied, "Tell them my name is **I** AM. (The Hebrew word for this is "**Yahweh**.") Tell them, 'Yahweh, the God of your fathers, the God of Abraham, the God of Isaac, and the God of Jacob, has sent me to you.' This is my name forever and this is the name I am to be remembered by through all generations. Go to

Pharaoh and say that the God of the Hebrews wants them to go into the desert for three days to offer sacrifices to him. I shall show my power and strike Egypt with all the wonders I am going to work there."

"But no one will believe me," said Moses.

God then gave Moses certain miraculous powers which would be signs to the people that he was sent by God.

But Moses still did not want to go. "Oh my Lord, you know that I speak slowly and stutter when I talk. Please send someone else," he said.

"Who gave man his mouth? Is it not I, Yahweh?" asked God. "I shall help you to speak and tell you what to say.

"I am sending you your brother, **Aaron**. He will go with you. You can tell him what you want to say and he will speak for you. I will teach you what to say and do."

So Moses and Aaron went to Egypt. They gathered the people of Israel together and performed all the signs that God had given them. The people believed and rejoiced that God was going to save them at last, and they bowed down and worshipped God.

Through Moses, God was starting to reveal himself more and more to his people.

Words to Know:

tribe   Moses
"I AM"   Yahweh   Aaron

Q. 29   *Does sin harm our relationship with God and our neighbor?*

Yes, sin harms our relationship with God and also with our neighbor. All sin hurts us and other people (CCC 1440).

Q. 30   *How did God communicate with Moses?*

God communicated with Moses through a burning bush and by filling Moses with God's word (Ex 3:2–4, 4:12).

Q. 31   *Does God choose the people whom men believe are best able to do his work or be his servants?*

No. To do his work or be his servants, God does not choose the people whom men believe best. We see that God chose Moses, even though he was not a good speaker and was fearful (Ex 4:10).

Q. 32   *By what name did God reveal himself to Moses, and through Moses to all people?*

God revealed himself to be "I AM," the God of Abraham, Isaac, and Jacob (Ex 3:14–15).

CHAPTER 9

God Saves His People

By strength of hand the LORD brought us out of Egypt, from the house of bondage.

Exodus 13:14

The Plagues

Then Moses and Aaron went to see Pharaoh. "Yahweh, the God of Israel, has said, 'Let my people go.' Let us make a journey of three days into the wilderness to offer sacrifice to our God," they announced.

"Who is Yahweh that I should listen to him? I know nothing of him," replied Pharaoh. "I can see that your people do not have enough work if they think that they have time to worship your God. We will have to give them even more work."

So the poor people's work became harder and longer. They were very angry with Moses and Aaron for starting the whole thing. "Oh Lord," cried Moses, "why did you ever send me? You have not delivered your people. In fact, things have become worse."

"I am Yahweh," God answered. "I will lay my hand on Egypt and with strokes of power lead out the sons of Israel. I will perform many signs and wonders. And all shall come to know that I am Yahweh when I stretch out my hand against Egypt. Now work the signs that I have given you." Moses and Aaron obeyed and again went before Pharaoh.

Even though they repeatedly performed marvels, Pharaoh hardened his heart. He still would not grant the request to let the people go.

Then, through Moses, to make Pharaoh relent, God sent ten **plagues**, each worse than the last, one after the other. In the first plague, all the waters were turned into blood. The second was the plague of frogs. The Nile River and the whole land swarmed with frogs, which came even into people's houses and into their beds. But Pharaoh still would not relent.

Then came the third plague. God told Moses to strike the sand with his rod. And when he did this, all the grains of sand in Egypt were turned into mosquitoes, which swarmed everywhere, biting animals and people. Pharaoh's men said, "This is the work of God," but still Pharaoh would not listen.

The fourth plague was the plague of flies. The fifth was the plague of the death of the Egyptians' livestock and cattle. The sixth was the plague of boils and sores on Egyptians' bodies. The seventh was the plague of hail. The eighth was the plague of locusts. The ninth was the plague of darkness. The children of Israel were the only ones not to suffer from these plagues. Despite these great signs, Pharaoh would not let God's people go.

The Passover

Finally, the tenth and worst plague was announced. God gave Moses this message to tell Pharaoh: "At midnight, Yahweh will pass through Egypt and leave the firstborn of every living creature dead, starting with your own first child right down to the firstborn of the Egyptians' cows. And there will be a great cry throughout all the land of Egypt, such as was never heard before. But none of the Hebrews' children or animals will die. After that, your people will come and beg us to leave."

Then God sent this message to the Hebrews through Moses: "On the fourteenth day of this month, every family must kill a perfect and spotless lamb from your flocks. You must take some of the blood and sprinkle it on your doorposts. Then you should roast the lamb and eat it with unleavened bread and bitter herbs. And while you are eating it, you must be dressed as though you are ready to leave at any minute; have your sandals on and your staff in your hand because you are going out of Egypt. Meanwhile, I will pass through Egypt and slay all the firstborn. But when I see the blood on your doorposts, I will pass over your house and your families will be spared. For this reason, I will call this night my **Passover** and from now on you shall eat this special meal every year to show that you remember that I rescued you from Egypt. It will be called the feast of Passover."

God also told them to consecrate every firstborn of the Israelites to him.

Free at Last

So the people of Israel prepared their first Passover meal. At midnight, God passed through and struck down all the firstborn of the Egyptians. Everywhere there was crying.

Pharaoh summoned Moses and Aaron that same night. "Take everything that is yours and go," he commanded with tears in his eyes, for his own son had died that night.

And so the Hebrews went out into the wilderness toward the Red Sea. But after they had gone, Pharaoh changed his mind. "Now who will serve us?" he asked. So he sent his army to bring them back.

When the Hebrews saw that the Egyptians were following them, they were very frightened. They could not get away because ahead of them was the Red Sea. "Are there not enough graves in Egypt that you bring us out here to die? Why did you ever make us leave Egypt?" the people complained to Moses.

"Have no fear! Stand firm and you will see that Yahweh will fight for you and save you," answered Moses. God instructed Moses to lift up his staff and stretch it over the sea. When he did this, a strong east wind started blowing. The waters were divided in two, and suddenly there was a dry path between the halves, leading to the other side. The people praised God and went along the path with a wall of water on either side.

The Egyptians chased them along the path through the sea. As soon as all the children of Israel had passed through and were safe on the other side, Moses held up his staff and the waters came crashing together again. All the Egyptians with their horses and chariots were swallowed up. The people of Israel saw this great act of God. They were safe and free, and they worshipped God and grew in faith. They sang in praise of God:

> The LORD is my strength and my song, and he has become my salvation; this is my God, and I will praise him, my father's God, and I will exalt him (Exodus 15:2).

Words to Know:

plague   Passover

46

Q. 33   *Why did God send plagues upon Egypt?*

God sent plagues upon Egypt to redeem Israel and to show the Egyptians that Yahweh is the one true God (Ex 6:7, 7:5).

Q. 34   *What is the Passover?*

The Passover is the great feast to remember when God delivered the Israelites from slavery out of Egypt (CCC 62, 1363, Ex 12:21–27).

Q. 35   *How did God finally free the Israelites from slavery to Pharaoh and the Egyptians?*

God allowed the Israelites to cross the Red Sea safely, while the Egyptians were swallowed up into the Red Sea (Ex 14:21–30).

CHAPTER 10

Great Things Happen on the Way to the Promised Land

And the LORD said to Moses, "Lo, I am coming to you in a thick cloud, that the people may hear when I speak with you, and may also believe you for ever." Then Moses told the words of the people to the LORD.

Exodus 19:9

Bread from Heaven

On the way to the Promised Land, the Hebrew people wandered for a long time in the desert and they often ran into difficulties. Through all the preceding events, God was preparing the chosen people for very great and important **revelations**. God always provided for them, but still they did not trust him enough. Every time something went wrong, they would complain about how they never should have followed Moses and Aaron.

The day came when all the food that they had brought with them ran out. The next morning, God sent a heavy dew to cover the ground. And when the dew evaporated, it left behind white flaky bread that tasted of honey; they called it "**manna**." What is more, God provided fresh manna each morning for the rest of the time that the Hebrews were in the desert.

The Ten Commandments

After three months the Hebrews arrived at the foot of Mount Sinai. God called to Moses from the mountain saying, "Tell the people of Israel, 'You have seen what I did to the Egyptians, and how I bore you on eagles' wings and brought you to myself. Now, therefore, if you will obey my voice and keep my covenant, you shall be my own possession. You shall be a kingdom of priests and a **consecrated** nation.' "

When Moses spoke these words to the people everyone answered, "All that Yahweh has said, we will do."

Then Moses climbed to the top of the mountain. A dense cloud covered it. Yahweh descended in the form of fire and spoke to him so that all people would hear and believe Moses. The whole mountain shook violently. The peo-

ple were not allowed to go near it, but they saw lightning flashes on Mount Sinai and heard peals of thunder and loud trumpet blasts, the sound of which made them tremble. To their eyes the glory of Yahweh seemed like a great fire on the mountaintop. Moses was gone for forty days and forty nights.

Then, one of the most important events in the history of the world took place. God gave Moses the **Ten Commandments** carved on stone tablets.

The Golden Calf

Meanwhile God's stubborn people became impatient and again doubted him. They went to Aaron and said, "Make us a god who will lead us. Moses is gone. We do not know what has become of him."

And so Aaron had their gold jewelry melted down and made into a statue of a calf.

"Tomorrow will be a feast in honor of the Lord," Aaron announced.

The next day, the people worshipped and sacrificed to the **golden calf**. God was angry to see that these people, for whom he had done so much, could forget him so quickly. He told Moses to go down from the mountain.

When Moses saw the people singing and dancing before the golden calf, he was so angry that he hurled down the tablets with the Ten Commandments that God had given his people, and the stone was shattered. Moses rebuked Aaron for letting the people get carried away. The golden calf was melted down and the people were punished for their sin, which was a grave sin of idolatry. Moses then wanted to make atonement for their sins, and he begged God to forgive them.

The Covenant Is Renewed

Once more, Moses climbed Mount Sinai to receive the Ten Commandments on stone tablets. He ate and drank nothing for forty days. This time God renewed the covenant that he had made so long ago with the descendants of Abraham. He said, "Go to the land that I swore I would give to Abraham, Isaac, and Jacob and to their descendants. I will send an angel on ahead of you." God also gave the people of

Israel many other laws to protect them and to be a sign that they were his chosen people.

When Moses finally came down the mountain, his face was radiant. It was shining so brightly from having spoken to God that he had to put a veil over it because people did not dare go near him. The mystery of God's greatness is impenetrable and his majesty is a thing of awe. God called his people to enter into a covenant with him.

The Ark of the Covenant

Under God's instructions, the people made a chest of fine wood called an ark. It was covered both inside and out with pure gold, and it had golden poles so that it could be carried. Inside the ark, they placed the stone tablets containing God's Ten Commandments. They called it the **Ark of the Covenant**.

The people also made a portable tent, and inside it they placed a **tabernacle**. This was where their priests would offer sacrifices to God on behalf of the people, and it would also be a sign of God's presence among them. Finally, they made a beautiful altar for the sacrifices and fine clothing for the priests.

The ark, the tabernacle, the vestments, and the altar were very carefully made following the instructions Moses received from God. These were all **sacred**. God also told Moses the exact way in which the holy ritual of sacrifice was to be performed. An animal victim was to be offered on the altar as an atonement for sins. Only Aaron and his descendants, the Levites, were allowed to be priests. They were especially chosen and consecrated for this.

The people of Israel continued travelling through the desert toward Canaan. The men carrying the Ark of the Covenant led the way, following a cloud which guided them.

Forty Years in the Desert

Finally one day, the Hebrews came to the edge of Canaan, the Promised Land. Moses sent out scouts on a secret mission. They were to see what Canaan looked like and who was living there.

The scouts came back with the report that the countryside was full of good fruits and vegetables. It really *was* a beautiful land. But the people living there, the Canaanites, were strong and fierce. Again, the people grumbled. "Let us get someone to lead us back to Egypt," they said.

God was so displeased with them that he decided that not one of these grumblers would enter the Promised Land. The people would wander in the desert for forty years until the last of them was dead, and then their children would enter Canaan. So for forty years the Jews remained in the desert and could not enter Canaan, the land that had so long ago been promised to the descendants of Abraham.

The Death of Moses

One day, God called to Moses, "Climb up into these mountains and look at the land I am going to give to the children of Israel. And after you have looked at it, you will die."

So Moses went up and looked at the Promised Land. And then he died up there on the mountain. Although the Hebrews had so often complained about him, they really loved

"The law of the LORD is perfect,
    reviving the soul;
the testimony of the LORD is sure,
    making wise the simple;
the precepts of the LORD are right,
    rejoicing the heart;
the commandment of the LORD is pure,
    enlightening the eyes."

Psalm 19:7–8

him and they were very sad that he had left them. They cried for a month.

Moses was a very great **prophet**. A prophet is someone whom God uses to speak to his people. Moses was very close to God, and God worked great miracles through him. Dramatic new revelations of God and the moral law were given through Moses to the Jewish people.

Words to Know:

revelation manna consecrated
Ten Commandments
golden calf Ark of the Covenant
tabernacle sacred prophet

Q. 36 *Why did God call the people of Israel to enter into a covenant with him?*

God called the people of Israel to enter into a covenant with him, so that they could come to know him and serve him as the one true God. God gathered his people to give them hope of salvation (CCC 54–64).

Q. 37 *What did the people of Israel have to do to keep the covenant?*

To keep the covenant, the people of Israel had to obey the Ten Commandments (CCC 62, 2061–62).

Q. 38 *Who must obey the Ten Commandments?*

All people must obey the Ten Commandments. God revealed them to Moses for all people (CCC 2072).

Q. 39 *What was manna?*

Manna was a bread rained down from heaven. God provided manna for his people in the desert so they would live (Ex 16:4–32).

Q. 40 *Why can we believe what Moses said and what God revealed through Moses?*

We can believe Moses because God descended upon Mount Sinai so all could see him in a dense cloud and hear him when he spoke to Moses. God did this so that all would believe in him forever (Ex 19:9).

Q. 41 *What was the Ark of the Covenant?*

The Ark of the Covenant was a chest lined with pure gold, in which the Ten Commandments were kept. In the Old Testament, God's presence remained with the Ark (Ex 25:8–10, Deut 10:5).

Q. 42 *Who were the priests of the people of Israel?*

Aaron and the Levites were the priests of the people of Israel (Ex 28:43–29:9).

CHAPTER 11

Life in the Promised Land

"You shall therefore keep all the commandment which I command you this day, that you may be strong, and go in and take possession of the land which you are going over to possess, and that you may live long in the land which the LORD swore to your fathers to give to them and to their descendants, a land flowing with milk and honey."

Deuteronomy 11:8

The Battle of Jericho

God appointed a man named **Joshua** to take Moses' place as leader, and before he died Moses laid his hands on Joshua to pass on God's wisdom. Joshua would be the one who would finally lead the Jews into the Promised Land.

The people who at that time were living in the land of Canaan were very sinful. The Bible describes the Canaanites as doing many evil things, even murdering their own children! God had been very patient with them, sending them little punishments to give them many chances to change. But they would not repent.

Finally, God gave the order for the people of Israel to cross the **Jordan River** and enter the Promised Land of Canaan—a beautiful land, flowing with milk and honey!

The Hebrews pitched camp outside the city of Jericho, which was on the edge of the Promised Land. Jericho was the first city that they would have to conquer. It had high and strong walls all around it, and when the people saw the Israelites, they closed all the entrances

and sealed up the city tightly. They had heard about the power of the God of Israel.

Joshua gave the command for the priests to carry the Ark of the Covenant around the city. The army marched in front, followed by seven priests carrying trumpets. The rest of the people of Israel followed them.

Each day for six days, they marched around the city. But on the seventh day, they marched

around it seven times. And on the seventh time around, Joshua ordered all the people to shout a mighty war cry. As they shouted, the walls of Jericho collapsed, and the Israelites stormed the city.

Under Joshua's leadership, the Hebrews soon conquered many other cities in the land of Canaan. Then they divided up the land into twelve parts. Each tribe received a part except for the descendants of Joseph, who received two parts, and the Levites, who were set apart as the priests of God. (These were ordained to offer sacrifices to God for the people of all the tribes.)

God Sends Samson

For many years, the Hebrews' biggest enemy was the **Philistines**. These powerful and warlike people were always attacking the children of Israel. In order to protect his people from the Philistines, God sent an angel to a woman from the tribe of Dan. "You will have a son who will rescue the children of Israel from the Philistines," the angel told her. "His strength will be in his hair, however, so he must never cut it."

Soon the woman had a son, whom she named **Samson**. Samson grew up to be very big and strong, and all the Philistines were afraid of him. Once, when many Philistines were attacking him, he grabbed the jawbone of a donkey and his strong arms started swinging. He struck down one thousand Philistines with that jawbone!

Then one day, Samson fell in love with a beautiful woman named **Delilah**. The Philistine leaders saw this as their chance to ruin Samson. They visited Delilah. "Find out where Samson's strength comes from, and we will each give you eleven hundred silver pieces," they said.

When Delilah was alone with Samson, she begged him and coaxed him several times to tell her the secret of his strength. Finally Samson gave in.

"If someone were to cut my hair, I would be as weak as any other man," confided Samson. So one night while Samson was asleep, Delilah brought in the Philistines and one of them cut Samson's hair.

Samson awoke, surrounded by his enemies. Fearless as he was, he started to push them away, but his power was gone. The Philistines blinded Samson and locked him up in prison. While he was there, no one noticed that his hair was starting to grow back.

Then one day, the Philistines decided to have a great festival in honor of their chief god, Dagon (who was half-man and half-fish) to thank him for helping them capture Samson. All the leaders of the Philistines were there. At one point, someone suggested that Samson be brought out so that they could make fun of him. The leaders sent a boy to fetch him.

"Let me lean against the pillars that support the roof of this house," Samson said to the boy. As soon as Samson's strong arms felt the pillars on either side of him, he cried, "Let me die with my enemies!" and he pushed with all his might. The house fell upon the leaders and all the people in it, killing Samson as well. In his death, Samson killed more Philistines than he had while he was alive.

This is how God rescued his people from the Philistines. We will see later how this story of one man giving his life for the people foreshadowed events to come.

Ruth

Judah's tribe (the tribe from which the Savior was going to come) lived in several cities, including Bethlehem. One year, when there was a famine in Bethlehem, a woman named **Naomi** went to live in the country of Moab with her husband and their two sons. While they were

there, both the sons married **pagan** women, Orpah and **Ruth**. (A pagan is a person who doesn't believe in the one, true God.) Then Naomi's husband and two sons died, leaving all three women alone.

Since the famine was over, Naomi decided to return to Bethlehem. So one day, she said to her two daughters-in-law, "May Yahweh be kind to you as you have been kind to those who have died and to me. But now go back to your parents' houses and may you both find new husbands." Orpah kissed Naomi goodbye and went home, but Ruth would not go. "Go after your sister-in-law. She has gone back to her people and her gods," Naomi said to her.

"Do not ask me to leave you," Ruth begged. "Wherever you go, I will go; wherever you live, I will live; your people shall be my people, and your God shall be my God; where you die, I will die, and there I will be buried. Not even death shall take you away from me!"

The two women then went to Bethlehem. When they finally arrived, they were very hungry. So Ruth went into the barley fields of one of Naomi's rich relatives named **Boaz**. As the workers reaped the grain, Ruth followed along behind, and she gathered up the pieces that fell to the ground for herself and Naomi to eat. Boaz, who happened to be in his fields that day, saw Ruth and asked who this beautiful woman was. He listened with admiration to the story of how kind she had been to her mother-in-law. He also heard how she had left her parents and her native land to live among people whose customs were strange to her and how she had come to worship the one, true God. Boaz eventually married Ruth, and they had a son named Obed, who became the father of **Jesse**, the father of David. It was from David that Jesus the Savior would come. Ruth freely chose the one, true God of the Jewish people. She was faithful and kind. For this she was chosen to continue the direct line of ancestors which led to King David and later to the birth of Christ.

Q. 43   *How did God bless and protect his people in the Promised Land?*
God blessed and protected his people in the Promised Land by giving them leaders, such as Joshua and Samson, holy women, such as Ruth and Naomi, and many prophets to prepare people for the Savior (CCC 64, Josh 1:1–9, Judg 13:24, Ruth 1:16).

"There shall come forth a shoot from the stump of Jesse, and a branch shall grow out of his roots. And the Spirit of the LORD shall rest upon him."

Isaiah 11:1–2

CHAPTER 12

A King for God's People

And the LORD said to Samuel, "Hearken to the voice of the people in all that they say to you; for they have not rejected you, but they have rejected me from being king over them.

1 Samuel 8:7

The Prophet Samuel

In the country of the tribe of Ephraim (Ephraim was one of Joseph's sons), there lived a woman named Hannah who was very sad because she was childless. Every year she and her husband would go to Shiloh, where the Ark was kept, to offer sacrifices to God before it. At these times Hannah would cry and pray for a son. "O Lord of Hosts!" she prayed through her tears, "if you will only give me a son, I will give him back to you to serve you for the rest of his life."

God finally sent Hannah a little boy, whom she named **Samuel**. When he was old enough, she brought him to Shiloh to help Eli, the priest who was in charge of the tabernacle. She gave him to God. Hannah would visit her son each year and bring him a beautiful little coat that she had made.

One night, when Samuel was sleeping near the Ark, he heard someone call, "Samuel! Samuel!" Thinking that Eli called, he ran to his bed.

"Here I am," he said.

"I did not call you, my son. Go back and lie down," said Eli.

Samuel lay down and heard his name called and ran to Eli again. Once more Eli sent him back to bed. The third time when he came running to Eli, Eli guessed that it was God who had called Samuel. "Go and lie down," he said, "and when the voice calls you, say, 'Speak, Lord, your servant is listening.' "

So Samuel lay down and the voice called him again. "Speak, Lord, your servant is listening," he replied.

Then Yahweh said, "I am going to punish Eli's family because his sons have blasphemed me and he did not stop them." It was true—Eli's sons *were* bad men. They treated God and their fellow men shamefully. They had done very wicked things—like stealing the offerings that people had brought for sacrifice. In fact, most of the people of Israel had turned away from God. Eli himself was a good man and he had spoken to his sons about their evil deeds, but he had not really done anything to stop them.

As Samuel grew up, his love for God grew and the Lord continued to speak to him. Soon all the children of Israel came to know that Samuel was a prophet.

The Ark Is Captured

At this time the Philistines were fighting the Hebrews again. At one battle, the Hebrews were defeated; four thousand Hebrews lay dead. "Let us bring the Ark into the battle," they cried. "That way God will come among us and we will win next time." So Eli's two sons brought the Ark from Shiloh and they all went into battle. At first the Philistines were afraid because they knew about the power of the God of Israel, but because of this they fought all the harder. And they not only killed thirty thousand Hebrews (among whom were Eli's sons), but they also captured the Ark!

However, a series of disasters were then brought down upon those who had stolen the Ark. Some of the Philistines who had taken it had set it up in the temple of their god, Dagon. The next day, they found the statue of Dagon lying face down before the Ark! They put their god back in his place, but the next morning

Dagon was back on the floor, and this time his head and his hands had been cut off!

The people in the city where Dagon's temple stood became very sick while the Ark was there. So they sent it to another city, but the same thing happened there, and many died. The Ark was moved from city to city with the same result until finally the people sent it back to the children of Israel.

Samuel explained to the Hebrews that the Ark was not a good luck charm. God would help them only if they returned to him with all their hearts. So the children of Israel **fasted** and said, "We have sinned against the Lord." Samuel prayed and offered sacrifice for them. And this time, when the Philistines attacked, God made his people victorious.

During Samuel's lifetime, the children of Israel always won their battles against the Philistines. Eventually, they stopped attacking the Hebrews and at last peace came to the children of Israel.

Request for a King

When Samuel grew old, he appointed his sons to take his place. But his sons were not good men: they took bribes, and they did not treat everyone fairly.

The old men of Israel then asked Samuel to appoint a king to govern the people of Israel. Samuel asked God what he should do. God answered, "By saying that they want a king, they are rejecting me as their king. From the day I brought them out of Egypt to this day, they have been abandoning me and serving other gods. Give them what they ask for but first warn them what a human king will be like."

So Samuel went to the people and told them that if they had a king he would take their sons for his armies and their daughters to be his cooks and bakers. Also, he would demand the best of their grain and olives, but the people refused to listen to these warnings. "No," they said, "we want to be like other nations and have a king who will lead us into battle." And so God told Samuel to appoint a king.

King Saul

Among the descendants of Benjamin (Joseph's younger brother) was a young man named **Saul** who was very tall and handsome.

One day Saul journeyed to another town. As he was walking, he met Samuel.

The Lord had told Samuel that on this day he would meet the man who should be king. When Samuel saw Saul, the Lord told him, "That is the man of whom I told you; he shall rule my people." So Samuel invited Saul to dine with him and stay overnight. The next morning he would tell him what was on his mind. The following day, Samuel anointed Saul's head with oil. Then he kissed him and said, "You shall be king over the Lord's people and save them from their enemies."

Samuel called all the tribes of Israel together and brought Saul before them. When the people saw Saul standing head and shoulders above them, they shouted, "Long live the king!"

Saul was a very good king at first. He was a good soldier, and, since he trusted and obeyed God, the children of Israel won their battles. But after a while Saul's heart began to turn away from God.

Once, after a battle, God had told Saul not to take anything from the defeated army. But this was too much for Saul to bear. He and his men gathered together the best sheep, oxen, lambs, and whatever else they thought was worth saving and brought it back with them.

God told Samuel what Saul had done. Samuel was very angry and went to look for Saul. When he found him, Saul said, "I did what the Lord commanded."

"But I hear the bleating of sheep and oxen. Why did you loot and take booty? That is not what the Lord commanded. Why did you not obey?" asked Samuel.

"We only brought them to sacrifice to God, and we didn't take anything else," lied Saul.

"The Lord cares more about obedience than about sacrifices. It is much better to obey than to sacrifice. Because you have rejected the commands from God, he has rejected you as king!" As Samuel walked away, Saul pleadingly held fast to his robe and accidentally tore it. "The Lord has torn the Kingdom of Israel from you this day and given it to a better man than you!" cried Samuel.

> "Because you have rejected the word of the LORD, he has rejected you from being king."
>
> 1 Samuel 15:23

> "Yahweh gives death and life . . . Yahweh judges the ends of the earth, he endows his king with power, he exalts the horn of his Anointed."
>
> Song of Hannah,
> 1 Samuel 2:6, 10

Words to Know:

Samuel   fast   Saul

Q. 44   *How did God show that Dagon was a false god?*
The statue of Dagon was found face-down before the Ark of the Covenant. Its head and hands were cut off as a sign that Dagon was a false god (1 Sam 5:4).

Q. 45   *Why was it wrong for Israel to want a king?*
It was wrong for Israel to want a king because God had claimed the people of Israel for his own nation—God was their king, and they were rejecting him (1 Sam 8:7).

Q. 46   *How was a king chosen for the Israelites?*
God sent Samuel the prophet to Saul, whom God had chosen. Samuel anointed Saul king of Israel (1 Sam 10:1).

CHAPTER 13

King David

The LORD said to Samuel, "How long will you grieve over Saul, seeing I have rejected him from being king over Israel? Fill your horn with oil, and go; I will send you to Jesse the Bethlehemite, for I have provided for myself a king among his sons."

1 Samuel 16:1

The Shepherd Boy

God told Samuel to go to Jesse (the grandson of Ruth), who lived in Bethlehem. One of Jesse's sons would be the new king of Israel. When Samuel arrived, Jesse had his sons come before him, one at a time. When Samuel saw the first one, who was very tall and handsome, he thought, "Surely this must be the one the Lord wants for king!"

But the Lord said to Samuel, "God does not see as man sees. Man looks at the outward appearance. God sees what is in a man's heart."

So seven of Jesse's sons passed before Samuel. But each time Samuel said, "The Lord has not chosen this one." Finally he asked, "Are all your sons here?"

"There is still the youngest," Jesse replied, "but he is out with the sheep." Samuel commanded that he be sent for. Then the youngest, a handsome, upright, young boy with fine eyes, arrived. His name was **David**.

God spoke to Samuel, "This is the one who is going to be the new king. Anoint him." So Samuel took his horn of oil and anointed

David. The Spirit of God was upon David from that day on.

At this time Saul was starting to lose his mind. An evil spirit was in him. His servants thought that some music would calm him. Word came to the palace about a young boy from Bethlehem who could play the harp beautifully. This was David. Saul sent for him, so David came to Saul and entered his service. David was such a good servant to Saul that Saul grew to love him. Whenever the evil spirit troubled Saul, David played the harp and Saul felt better.

Goliath

One day, while the men of Israel were preparing for war, they saw a huge giant of a man in heavy armor come forward from the Philistine camp. "Choose a man from your side," challenged this man, whose name was **Goliath**. "If he is able to kill me, we Philistines will be your slaves, but if I kill him, you shall be *our* slaves." The Hebrews were terrified!

When David heard Goliath's challenge, he went to Saul. "I will fight Goliath," he said.

"You are only a boy, and Goliath has been in the army since he was a child," Saul replied.

"But I have killed lions and bears to protect my sheep. And this Philistine, Goliath, is like one of the wild beasts because he is attacking the armies of the living God."

Saul gave David his own armor, his own sword, and a bronze helmet. David found that he could not move in all that heavy armor, however, so he went to meet Goliath without it. He had his slingshot in his hand. As he crossed a brook he picked up five smooth stones and put them into his shepherd's bag.

When Goliath saw David coming out to fight against him, he was insulted that the Israelites would send out a young boy. He cursed David by his gods. David called out, "You fight me armed with a sword, spear, and javelin, but I fight you in the name of the Lord of Hosts, the God of the armies of Israel, whom you have defied. Today, this God will help me defeat you. I will cut off your head so that all the earth will know that there is a God in Israel. It is not by the sword that God gives the victory, for it is God who is Lord of the battle."

Goliath came toward David, and David ran to meet him. David pulled out one of the smooth stones and wrapped his slingshot around it. He let the stone fly, and it struck Goliath's forehead and knocked him out. David ran over and, drawing Goliath's own sword, cut

off his head. When the Philistines saw that their champion was dead, they took flight.

There was great rejoicing among the children of Israel. The women came out to meet King Saul singing with cries of joy: "Saul has killed his thousands, and David his ten thousands!"

This song made Saul very jealous. "David has more glory than I have," he muttered to himself. "What is left for him to take but my kingdom?" The next day, when an evil spirit again came upon him, he tried to kill David with his spear, but David was able to get away.

In Hiding

David became a great commander of Saul's army, and all the people loved him. Finally, Saul could stand it no longer. "I am going to kill David," he confided to his son, Jonathan. But Jonathan also loved David, and he helped him to escape. David spent the next few years with a small band of men, hiding from Saul's army in mountains and caves.

One night, David and one of his men crept into Saul's camp. They found Saul fast asleep with his spear nearby. "God has arranged this," whispered his friend. "Let me kill him with his own spear."

But David stopped him. "No," he said. "Saul

battle but the prophet Samuel had died and he was all alone. So he went to the house of a sorceress. "Bring up Samuel from the dead so that I can talk to him," he said.

Suddenly, an old man wrapped in a robe appeared in the room. Saul recognized Samuel at once and bowed down. "Why have you disturbed me?" Samuel asked.

"I am so worried," replied Saul. "I do not know what to do about the Philistines. Please tell me what to do."

"Since God has turned away from you, why do you ask me? God has torn the kingdom from you and given it to David. Furthermore, you and your sons will all be dead with me tomorrow!" And it happened just as Samuel had said. The next day, when the Philistines attacked, Saul and his sons, including Jonathan, were caught and killed.

King David

As soon as David became king, he and his men attacked the great city of **Jerusalem**, which had been inhabited by people known as the Jebusites. David announced that this city would bear his name: he called it the **City of David**.

Before David did anything else, he went with the children of Israel to bring the Ark into Jerusalem. He had such deep reverence for the Ark of the Covenant, which was sacred. He thought he was unworthy to bring it, so he first offered sacrifices. He was delighted that the Ark was going to be set up in his own city. He and all the House of Israel danced before the Ark, singing songs and playing harps and cymbals, as they carried it into Jerusalem.

As they came into the city, David's wife, Michal, looked out of the window and saw her husband dancing before the Ark. She thought this was foolish of David, and she told him he was making a fool of himself in front of his servants.

is still the king, God's anointed one. The Lord himself will punish him if he wants. *We* would do wrong to kill him. But we will take his spear and this jar of water."

When they returned to their own camp, David called out to the army, "Why aren't you watching over your king? Look, here is his spear and here is the jar of water that was at his head!"

"Is that your voice, my son, David?" asked Saul.

"It is my voice, my lord, O king. What have I done that you are trying to kill me?"

"I have sinned, my son, David. I will never harm you again since you have spared my life." David knew that Saul would change his mind and try to kill him again, so he went to live in the land of the Philistines for a while.

The Death of Saul

Meanwhile, Saul was getting ready to fight a large army of Philistines, and he was very frightened. He wanted to ask God about the

"I was dancing for the Lord, not for them. I *will* dance before Yahweh and demean myself even more," David replied.

Throughout his life David composed many songs. They are called **Psalms**. He was an excellent king who was just and good. The Hebrews loved him, and the Lord blessed him.

Bathsheba

In the spring, instead of going to war, David remained in Jerusalem. One evening as he was walking on the roof of his palace, he saw a very beautiful woman named **Bathsheba**. David had her brought to him, and he wanted to marry her at once. When he found out that she was already married to a soldier named Uriah he arranged to have Uriah placed up in the front line of battle. And it happened, just as David had planned, that Uriah was killed in battle. So David brought Bathsheba to the palace to be his wife.

God was very displeased with David. He sent the prophet **Nathan** to him, and Nathan told David this story: "Once there was a rich man and a poor man. The rich man had many sheep, but the poor man had only one little lamb. This lamb grew up with him and his children, and he loved it very much. One day, the rich man had company and, instead of killing one of his many lambs for dinner, he killed the poor man's only lamb and served it."

At this David grew very angry and cried, "As the Lord lives, the rich man who had no pity and did this deserves to die!"

Nathan replied, "You are the man. Yahweh the God of Israel says this: 'I have given you so much. And yet you have killed Uriah and have taken his wife. Why have you shown contempt for Yahweh, doing what displeases him? Your punishment will be that wars against you will never end.' "

David suddenly saw what he had done. "I have sinned against the Lord," he said. God forgave David because he was very sorry for his sin. David did not have to die for this sin, but he did have to suffer his punishment.

David then composed a Psalm which the Church prays even in our day (Psalm 51), because it expresses deep and perfect contrition and true love of God. David delighted in God. God chose David to be an ancestor of Jesus Christ, our Savior.

"Have mercy on me, O God,
  according to thy steadfast love;
  according to thy abundant mercy blot
    out my transgressions.
Wash me thoroughly from my iniquity,
  and cleanse me from my sin!

For I know my transgressions,
  and my sin is ever before me.
Against thee, thee only, have I sinned,
  and done that which is evil in thy
    sight. . . .

Behold, thou desirest truth in the
    inward being;
  therefore teach me wisdom in my
    secret heart.
Purge me with hyssop, and I shall
    be clean;
  wash me, and I shall be whiter
    than snow. . . .

Create in me a clean heart, O God,
  and put a new and right spirit
    within me.
Cast me not away from thy presence,
  and take not thy holy Spirit from
    me. . . ."

Psalm 51:1–4, 6–7, 10–11

He shall cry out to me, 'Thou art my Father, my God, and the Rock of my salvation.'

And I will make him the first-born, the highest of the kings of the earth.

Psalm 89:26–27

Words to Know:

David   Goliath   Jerusalem
City of David   Psalms
Bathsheba   Nathan

Q. 47 *Why was David made king, even though Saul was still alive?*

David was made king, even though Saul was still alive, because God rejected Saul for his faithlessness (1 Sam 15:23).

Q. 48 *What did David show the Israelites when he beat Goliath with only a slingshot?*

David showed the Israelites that it was God who fought for Israel and defeated Goliath (1 Sam 17:46).

Q. 49 *How did David displease God?*

David displeased God by taking Uriah's wife, Bathsheba, for himself, which is a grave sin. After doing this, David had Uriah killed so that he could marry Bathsheba (CCC 2268, 2336).

Q. 50 *Did David repent of his sin before God and man?*

Yes, David repented of his sin before God and man, and did penance (2 Sam 12:13)

Q. 51 *Did God make a covenant with David?*

Yes, God made a covenant with David and established the throne of his kingdom forever (2 Sam 7:13).

CHAPTER 14

King Solomon and The Promise of a New King

He shall build a house for my name, and I will establish the throne of his kingdom for ever.

2 Samuel 7:13

Solomon the Wise

David eventually died and was buried in his own city of Jerusalem. His son **Solomon** became the new king. Solomon loved God very much and followed his commandments. One night Solomon had a dream: "What would you like me to give you?" asked God.

"Oh, my Lord!" replied Solomon. "I do not know how to be king. Please give me, your servant, wisdom so that I can rule over your people. And help me to know good from evil."

God was so pleased that Solomon asked for these gifts, instead of a long life or riches, that he rewarded him with great wisdom. Since the time of Adam and Eve there had never been anyone as wise as Solomon! And besides this, God also gave him what he had not asked for—riches and a long life.

Almost at once, Solomon needed to use his wisdom. One day two women came to him. "My lord," began one of the women, "we live together and both of us had babies. Hers died one night and, while I was asleep, she switched the babies!"

But the other woman argued, "*My* child is alive and *hers* is dead."

What a dilemma for Solomon! How could he discover which woman was lying? Then he commanded, "Bring me a sword." When the sword was brought in, Solomon ordered, "Now cut the child in two and give half to each woman."

The first woman cried, "Oh, no, my Lord. Give her the baby, only do not kill him!"

"No, let us divide him!" shouted the second woman.

Now Solomon knew the true mother of the child. He knew that a real mother would not want her child killed, even if she had to give him to someone else. And so the first woman was given the child.

The wisdom of Solomon became known throughout the whole land. People came from all over the earth to hear his wise words and to ask his advice. To thank him for his good advice, they brought him gifts of silver, gold, spices, and horses. Soon he was very rich.

The Temple in Jerusalem

Solomon ordered that a magnificent **temple** be built in Jerusalem where the Ark would be kept and where God would be worshipped. After many years, it was finally finished. It was beautiful! The walls were of fragrant olive and cedar wood and the entire temple was covered

with gold. The Ark, containing the stone tablets that Moses had received on Mount Sinai, was brought in. The king blessed all the people and there was a great celebration, which lasted for seven days.

The Foolish Solomon

Solomon's kingdom grew and grew. He married the daughters of several **gentile** kings, including the daughter of the Pharaoh of Egypt. (A gentile is someone who is not a Jew.) These princesses brought Solomon land as part of their marriage arrangements. It was a very peaceful time, since Solomon became related through marriage to many of the Hebrews' former enemies.

But these wives proved to be Solomon's downfall. As he grew older, he let them turn his heart away from God. He built altars and offered sacrifices to the gods of his gentile wives. God saw that Solomon did not love him the way he used to. So he decided that Solomon's son would not be king, but that the kingship would go to someone else.

The Prophet Isaiah

In Jerusalem, not too long after Solomon died, a child was born named **Isaiah**, which means "Yahweh is salvation." One day, when Isaiah was older, he was praying in the temple. Suddenly he saw a vision of God sitting on a throne and surrounded by angels who were chanting, "Holy, Holy, Holy is the Lord of Hosts; the whole earth is full of his glory!" This vision was so great and beautiful that Isaiah was overcome by his own sinfulness. "Woe is me!" he cried.

But then one of the angels flew down to him and touched his lips with a burning coal. "This has touched your lips," he said. "Your sins are forgiven."

Then God himself spoke to Isaiah. He wanted to send a message to the people of Israel. "Whom shall I send, and who will go for us?" he asked gently.

"Send me!" answered Isaiah, eager to be of help.

So Isaiah became God's great prophet to deliver his word to the people of Israel. (There were also many other important prophets in Israel.) Much of the time Isaiah talked of how the people needed to repent of their sins and turn back to God. He also told them of a spe-

cial servant of God who would come to save them. This was the one who had been promised ages ago to Adam and Eve. The Jews had a word for this Savior. They called him the "**Messiah**" or the **Christ**, which means the "Anointed One."

Isaiah predicted that this servant of God would be a descendant of Jesse and David. He also said that wonderful things would happen when he was born. The whole earth would be filled with peace and happiness! Because of this, the people were expecting the Messiah to be a powerful king, like David or Solomon, who would make them a strong nation once again.

But Isaiah also told of strange and unheard of sufferings of God's servant the Messiah. He

"Behold, a young woman shall conceive and bear a son and shall call his name Immanuel." [Immanuel means "God with us."]

Isaiah 7:14

would be despised and rejected, slapped and spit upon. He would suffer for the sins of the people and, by his sufferings, he would heal them. Finally, he would even offer up his life for his people. These **prophecies** were written down (we have them in the book of the Bible named after Isaiah), and they were studied long after his death. They seemed difficult to understand, however. What would the new king be like?

Words to Know:

Solomon   temple   gentiles   Isaiah   Messiah   Christ   prophecy

> I gave my back to the smiters,
>   and my cheeks to those who pulled out the beard;
> I hid not my face from shame and spitting.
>
> Isaiah 50:6
>
> But he was wounded for our transgressions,
>   he was bruised for our iniquities;
> upon him was the chastisement that made us whole,
>   and with his stripes we are healed.
>
> Isaiah 53:5

PART TWO

A.D. In the Year Of Our Lord

CHAPTER 15

The Final King

As it is written in the book of the words of Isaiah the prophet, "The voice of one crying in the wilderness: Prepare the way of the Lord, make his paths straight."

Luke 3:4

Exile to Babylon

Partly as a result of Solomon's sins, after his death the tribes of Israel were soon divided. Ten of the tribes had their own king, and they named their country Israel. The other two tribes named their country after the tribe of Judah, which was Solomon's tribe. The towns of Jerusalem and Bethlehem were both in the Kingdom of Judah.

As time went by, the children of Israel turned away from God more and more. Not only did the two kingdoms fight with their neighbors but they began to fight with each other as well. God sent many prophets to turn the people back to him again but the people would not listen. In fact, when the Hebrews did not like what the prophets said, they often killed them. The two kingdoms grew weaker and weaker.

One day, the king of Babylon, Nebuchadnezzar, conquered Jerusalem. His armies ran through the city, destroying everything. The beautiful Temple was destroyed and its treasures were carried off. The king of Judah and many Hebrews were taken away to Babylon to be the servants of King Nebuchadnezzar.

A Time of Waiting

After a long time, some of the Jews from the Kingdom of Judah were allowed to return to Jerusalem and rebuild the royal city of David. They repaired the temple which had been in ruins for so long, but they did not live in peace. Their enemies moved in and took control of Jerusalem. From the prophet Isaiah and others, the people knew that God was going to send them a Messiah, a savior, a new king, who would be a descendant of David. But the king seemed to be a long time in coming.

Finally, Caesar, the emperor of Rome, conquered the Kingdom of Judah. He appointed a man named Herod, who was not a descendant of David, to be ruler of the Kingdom of Judah. Where was the king who would save the Jews?

John the Baptist

At last, word came to the people of Jerusalem of a man who was living in the desert by the Jordan River outside of Jerusalem. His name was **John the Baptist**, and he was telling people to be sorry for their sins and to do

penance in order to be ready for the new king, who was about to come.

He was dressed in a rough garment of camel hair, and he lived in the desert, eating nothing but wild honey and locusts.

John was the greatest of the prophets sent by God to help the people of Israel prepare for Jesus, their new King. The people came out to him in the desert and stood in the Jordan River (which was the river the Hebrews had crossed into the Promised Land). John baptized them there in the Jordan River. For this reason, he came to be called the Baptist or the Baptizer. This baptism or washing was a sign that they were willing to give up their sins and turn to God with all their hearts.

The simple and humble people grew to love John because he was holy and good, but some of the people who came to hear him disliked him. This was because he could be very fierce at times. He could see that some of those who came to him really did not want to try to love God and give up their sins. He told them the truth, and they did not like to hear it.

Soon John became famous and many came from Jerusalem and all of Judea (the area of the Kingdom of Judah) to be baptized. Others just came to see what all the commotion was about. Many thought that maybe this man in the ragged garments was the new king.

"Are you the one who was promised to us?" asked some of the priests of the tribe of Levi.

"I am not. There is one coming after me who is greater than I and whose sandal I am not worthy to undo!" John replied. "I baptize only with water but he will baptize you with the Holy Spirit and with fire!"

God Makes the New King Known

Then one day, John's cousin, Jesus, a descendant of David from the tribe of Judah, came to be baptized. John did not want to baptize him. For the Jews, baptism was a sign of repentance for sins and John knew that Jesus was without sin. "It is I who should be baptized by you," John said humbly, but Jesus insisted, and so John baptized him.

At this the heavens opened, the Holy Spirit came down in the form of a dove, and the voice of God was heard, "This is my beloved Son, in whom I am well pleased." In this way, God was showing the people of Israel who the new King was.

The one who would crush the power of evil had arrived and was ready to begin his work!

Everything, from the first moment of creation, had been leading up to this greatest and last King, the Messiah, Jesus.

A Different Kind of King

For many people in Israel this was a big surprise. Right from the beginning, this new King did not appear to be like the other kings of Israel. "My Kingdom does not belong to this world," he said. He was poor and did not live in a palace. He went about the countryside of Judea with some fishermen whom he had chosen to be his special friends or disciples, spending a lot of time eating with sinners and with the common and poor people. Could this be the one who had been promised to the Hebrews? He was not at all what many of them had expected!

Words to Know:

John the Baptist

Q. 54 *Who was the greatest of the prophets sent by God to help the people of Israel prepare for the coming of Jesus?*

Saint John the Baptist was the greatest of the prophets sent by God to help the people of Israel prepare for the coming of Jesus (CCC 523).

Q. 55 *When John baptized Jesus, how was the new King known?*

When John baptized Jesus in the Jordan, the heavens opened, the Holy Spirit appeared as a dove, and the voice of God the Father was heard saying: "This is my beloved Son, with whom I am well pleased" (CCC 535, Mt 3:13–17).

". . . the kingdom of God has come upon you."

Matthew 12:28

CHAPTER 16

An Invitation to Heaven

He who believes and is baptized will be saved.

Mark 16:16

A Special Invitation

With Jesus Christ, a new part of the Bible begins—the most important part—because Jesus came not just to be king of the Jews but to be King of the whole world. He came to bring his Kingdom of truth and love, of justice and peace, of holiness and grace.

Very likely, not too long after you were born, you received a special invitation to Christ's Kingdom. This Kingdom comes to us through the Church and, in a sense, it is the Church. Jesus invited you to become a member of it through your baptism. Jesus wanted you to become a Catholic Christian because then you could get all the help you need to do his will on earth and to be with him forever in heaven. So your parents took you to church and you were baptized. From that moment on you have received the help you need to travel toward God on earth on your way to heaven.

Now that you are a Catholic, God is inviting you to be more his own every minute. He is inviting you right this very minute to continue your pilgrimage on the road to heaven by always trying to love him and others.

When you receive an invitation to go to a party, you are not forced to go. You go because you want to. Neither were your parents forced to accept God's invitation to have you baptized. They did it because they love you and want your happiness now and forever. And so when Christ invites you to follow him and then to come to heaven, he does not force you. He lets you make up your own mind to say "yes" or "no."

Human Beings Are Special Creatures

Do you remember the story of how God made the first man? He made a body out of the dust of the earth and then breathed a soul into it which made the man come alive. The human person is both body and soul. The body will die one day, but the soul will live forever. A human being is above the animals because he has an immortal soul which can understand things—like math—and has a free will. The soul is the spiritual part of man, by which he lives, understands, and is free. The soul allows man to know, love, and serve God.

Free Will

This power to make up our minds to do or not do something is a special gift from God. It is called **free will**. God made us in his own im-

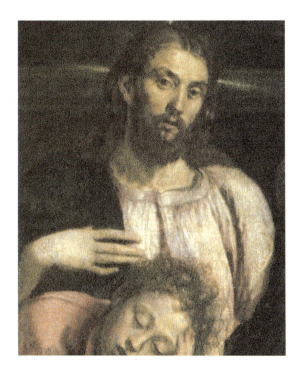

Moses and the Commandments

Are you wondering how to say "yes" to Jesus' invitation to heaven? God gave us ten ways to do this. God gave the Ten Commandments to Moses on Mount Sinai because he knew that only by following them would people be truly happy and at peace. So in his great love for the children of Israel, God gave them the Ten Commandments.

God expected the Jews to have great reverence for these special laws, and they did. The Ten Commandments were considered so important that the beautiful Ark of the Covenant was built just for them!

Jesus and the Ten Commandments

Since Jesus was a Jew, he grew up like a Jewish boy, learning the Commandments from Mary and Joseph. When Jesus was growing up, however, there were many people who thought that they could be good by just following the exact words of the Commandments without doing what they really meant. This made them look as if they were holy and good, but their hearts were far away from God. These men made it difficult for others too. People became confused about how to follow God's laws. So when Jesus became a man and started to teach the people, he wanted to show them what the Commandments were really all about.

Loving God and Others

The Commandments were all about love— Christ said that what our Heavenly Father wants most of all is for us to love him with all our *hearts* and with all our *souls* and with all our *minds* and with all our *strength*. And then he said that we must love others as we love ourselves. By saying this, Christ wants us to know that if we really want to be good, we must put our hearts into following the Commandments.

age and likeness. Human beings are different from animals because animals do not have free will. Because we can think, we can use our minds to make a choice. A dog or cat cannot make choices the way we can. For example, if a dog is hungry, he will eat when you give him food, but even if you are hungry, you can still decide not to eat.

We Will Say Yes

God wants us to show him that we love him. He will never force us, but he waits for our answer and even helps us to say "yes" to him by giving us his grace. Our choice, which we must make every day, is either to say "no" like Adam and Eve or to be like Abraham and Mary, who said "yes" to God. And, although we have the power to say "no" to God, once we see that something is wrong and would offend God (and besides would make us very unhappy), we will want always to say "yes!" God made us to be with him, so when we say "yes" to God, we will be happy and truly free.

The first three Commandments tell us how to love God. The other seven tell us how to love others. In the next chapter we will talk about the three ways to love God, or the first three Commandments.

1. I am the LORD your God: you shall not have strange gods before me.

2. You shall not take the name of the LORD your God in vain.

3. Remember to keep holy the LORD's Day.

4. Honor your father and your mother.

5. You shall not kill.

6. You shall not commit adultery.

7. You shall not steal.

8. You shall not bear false witness against your neighbor.

9. You shall not covet your neighbor's wife.

10. You shall not covet your neighbor's goods.

Q. 56 *What is man?*

Man is a reasoning being composed of body and soul (CCC 355, 362).

Q. 57 *What is the soul?*

The soul is the spiritual part of man, by which he lives, understands, and is free. The soul allows man to know, love, and serve God (CCC 356, 363).

Q. 58 *Does man have free will?*

Man has free will because he is able to choose to do or not to do a thing, or to do one thing rather than another (CCC 311).

Q. 59 *Can man do evil and be truly free?*

No, man cannot do evil and be truly free. Though God allows us to choose between good and evil, to be truly free we must choose to follow the good and say "yes" to God (CCC 1733).

Q. 60 *What are the Commandments of God?*

The Commandments of God are the moral laws that God gave to all mankind through Moses on Mount Sinai in the Old Testament, and which Jesus Christ perfected in the New Testament (CCC 1962, 1968).

Q. 61 *What are our duties toward God and neighbor?*

Our duties toward God and neighbor are to love God and neighbor. The first three Commandments tell us how to love God. The other seven Commandments tell us how to love our neighbor (Mt 22:38–40, CCC 1822–24).

"For this is the love of God, that we keep his commandments."

1 John 5:3

CHAPTER 17

Road Signs Along the Way

You shall love the LORD your God with all your heart, and with all your soul, and with all your might.

Deuteronomy 6:5

1. *I am the LORD your God: you shall not have strange gods before me.*

The One True God

Why do you think that God was displeased when the Israelites worshipped the golden calf and when the wise Solomon was foolish enough to honor his wives' gods? It was because there is only *one* God and he alone is worthy of worship.

Can you imagine what it would be like if you gave someone many things but, instead of thanking you, he thanked someone else for them? It would not be right or true. God has done more than give us things. He created us and he keeps us in existence every second! We depend upon him for everything. It is not right or truthful to worship someone or something else for those things, which God alone has given us.

But God was telling the people of Israel that they should do more than just keep from worshipping false gods. Because God is who he is, we must give proper worship to him as the one true God and Creator of all that exists.

Our False Gods

Although the Jews lived in a time when people worshipped **idols** and golden statues, most people in the world today do not worship statues. There is another way of worshipping gods other than the one true God. This is when we treat our possessions like gods or make them more important than God. We want more and more money and possessions to keep for ourselves, and sometimes we may even do wrong things to get them. We may be so stingy with them—not wanting to share them with others—that we make them into false gods. Do you refuse to let your brother or sister ride your bicycle or come into your room? Or perhaps we do things that we know are wrong just to be popular or so others won't laugh at us. This is making a god out of our popularity. God has given us so many gifts and he wants us to enjoy them. But we must be careful not to let these things take place over him in our lives.

Believing in God

The First Commandment also tells us to believe the things that God has told us about himself, about ourselves, and about his Church. God gave you the gift of faith at your baptism so that you are able to believe all that he tells you.

But how can you believe in someone or in the things that he tells you, if you don't know anything about him or about those things? So in the First Commandment, God tells you to learn about him and what he has to say to you. You learn those things from what the Catholic Church teaches, that is, by paying attention right here to what your religion teacher and books have to say. You are learning some of the things that God wants you to know right now!

Praying to God

If we really follow the First Commandment, we will pray to God every day. What are some of the reasons people do not pray? Some do not think that God really has any control over their lives. Others do not believe in him enough or do not love him enough. Some people do not pray unless they are frightened or want something very badly.

But God thinks that our **prayers** are *very* important so he often waits until we ask him. He wants us to show that we trust him. If we received all that we want without asking, we would probably forget who really gave them to us, and we would start to think that we had gotten them all by ourselves.

Holy God, holy strong One, holy Immortal One, have mercy on us.

Byzantine chant

Prayer means talking with God. You talk with him so that you can get to know him better, to love him, to adore him, to thank him for what he has given you, to tell him you are sorry for what you have done wrong, or to ask him for something. God will answer by giving you his grace and by granting your prayers, perhaps in unexpected ways. You can pray anywhere or anytime because God always listens.

Does praying sound hard? It will help if, before you begin your prayers, you remember that God really *is* there and really *wants* to hear what you are going to tell him or ask him. He wants to give good things to you and the people you love. He is just waiting to be asked. Above all, he wants your love.

Sometimes, however (although certainly not every time!), God knows that what you ask for would not be best for you or for someone else. So in his great love for you, he uses another way than the one you were expecting to answer your prayer.

2. *You shall not take the name of the LORD your God in vain.*

Respect for God's Name

Sometimes the way we talk about people tells others just what we think of them. If you are angry with a person, the way you talk about him will let others know how you feel. On the other hand, you talk about someone you like in a nice way.

How much more should we talk with the greatest care about God who is all holy! God wants us always to use his name with the greatest **respect**, and this is what he tells us in the Second Commandment when he says, "Do not take the name of the Lord, your God, in vain." "In vain" means for no good purpose or reason. If we start using God's name carelessly, we can forget just who he is.

The Jewish people had such deep **reverence** for the greatness and majesty of the all-holy

God that they would not even say the word "Yahweh" but said "the Lord" instead. This should give us an idea of the reverence due to God. It makes us all the more thankful that we are allowed to call this great God "Our Father," as Jesus taught us.

Prayer

One special way that God wants us to use his name is in prayer. We often begin our prayers, "in the *Name* of the Father, and of the Son, and of the Holy Spirit" and end them by using the *name* of "Christ, Our Lord."

Vows

There are other ways in which we can and should use God's name. Sometimes we use it to make a promise to God, which is called a vow. To break such a promise would be to use God's name in vain because we should not make promises to God and then treat them so lightly that we break them. Examples of a vow would be the vow married people make to each other and to God that they will be faithful to each other for the rest of their lives or that religious sisters, brothers, and priests make when they vow to live a life of special service to God and to others.

Using God as Your Witness

Sometimes we call on God to witness that what we say is true. We call this swearing an oath. Swearing is necessary in courtrooms and under other special circumstances but it would be wrong to call God to witness the truth of our statements without a good reason or if what we are saying is not true. If you find yourself using God's name to convince your friends that you are telling them the truth or saying things like "I swear to God," you should stop doing it. Your honest word should be enough.

Other Sins

Often when someone uses God's name because he is angry or excited, people say that he is "swearing" or "cursing." Cursing means to call down evil on someone. **Blasphemy** means using God's name disrespectfully, carelessly, or even hatefully. These are sins against the Second Commandment.

Holy Persons, Places, and Things

Not only must we treat God's name with great respect, but we should also respect those holy persons, places, and things that are connected with him. For example, we must be careful to talk about Mary, the Mother of God, and all of God's saints with respect.

Do you remember how God told Moses to take off his shoes when he came near the burning bush? This was a sign of respect because he was walking on holy ground—God was there in a special way. We must respect our holy places too. When you are in church, as a sign of reverence for Jesus, who is in the tabernacle, you should genuflect. If it is necessary to speak, you should do so in a low voice, and you should also walk quietly, because you do not want to disturb others who are praying.

3. Remember to keep holy the LORD's Day.

Which day is the Lord's Day? For the children of Israel, it was Saturday. This was their **Sabbath**, which means "rest" day. From sundown on Friday to sundown on Saturday all work would stop and people would spend time with God by praying to him and learning about

> "Ask, and it will be given you; seek and you will find; knock and it will be opened to you."
>
> Matthew 7:7

him. It was also a time for recreation with family and friends.

But there came one special Sabbath, when Jesus was lying dead in a tomb for the whole day. He rose the next day, Sunday. Because of that, his followers changed the Lord's Day from Saturday to Sunday.

Since we are followers of Jesus, Sunday is our day of rest. The Third Commandment teaches us to keep Sunday holy. Above all, we must participate in the Mass on the Lord's Day. At Mass we come together with others who believe in Christ and follow him to honor and praise God and to unite ourselves to the Holy Sacrifice offered by the priest.

After Mass, there are many things that you can do to make Sunday a holy and special day. Some people have a special Sunday breakfast or dinner for the whole family.

No matter how you celebrate Sunday, the point to remember is that any work that does not need to be done should be put off until another day. Sunday is a day of rest and prayer and should be dedicated to God.

Along with Sundays, there are other days in the year called **Holy Days of Obligation** which we treat like Sundays. On these days we participate at Mass and we avoid any unnecessary work. Even if you have to go to school on one of these days, you should do your best to make it holy. Ask your teacher to tell you which days these are.

Have you learned more about how to love God than you knew before? If you have, you have learned that from now on you should try to be someone who: 1) puts God first by praying to him every day and learning about him and the things he has told us through his Church; 2) always uses God's name with respect; and 3) makes Sunday and other holy days special days of worship of God, especially by assisting at Mass.

Words to Know:

idol prayer respect
reverence blasphemy Sabbath
Holy Day of Obligation

Holy Days of Obligation in the United States

In addition to Sunday, the days to be observed as holy days of obligation in the Latin Rite dioceses of the United States of America, in conformity with canon 1246, are as follows:

January 1, the solemnity of Mary, Mother of God;
Thursday of the Sixth Week of Easter, the solemnity of the Ascension;
August 15, the solemnity of the Assumption of the Blessed Virgin Mary;
November 1, the solemnity of All Saints;
December 8, the solemnity of the Immaculate Conception;
December 25, the solemnity of the Nativity of Our Lord Jesus Christ.

Q. 62 *What are we told to do by the First Commandment?*

The First Commandment tells us to believe in God, to trust him, to pray to him, and to love him above all other things (CCC 2134).

Q. 63 *What does the First Commandment forbid?*

The First Commandment forbids the worship of false gods and ignorance of God's plan (CCC 2110).

Q. 64 *What is prayer?*

Prayer means talking with God. Prayer is the lifting up of the soul to God in order to know him better, to adore him, to tell him we are sorry, and to ask him for what we need (CCC 2098).

Q. 65 *What are we told to do by the Second Commandment?*

The Second Commandment tells us to honor the name of God with the greatest respect and to fulfill the vows and promises we have made (CCC 216).

Q. 66 *What is forbidden by the Second Commandment?*

The Second Commandment forbids us to use God's name without respect; to blaspheme God, the most holy Virgin Mary, the saints, or holy things; or to swear oaths that are false, not necessary, or wrong in any way (CCC 2146–49).

Q. 67 *What are we told to do by the Third Commandment?*

The Third Commandment teaches us to keep Sunday holy. We do this by assisting at Mass and dedicating the day to God with our prayer and resting from work (CCC 2168, 2180).

Q. 68 *What is forbidden by the Third Commandment?*

The Third Commandment forbids us to do any unnecessary work on Sundays and Holy Days of Obligation (CCC 2184–85).

"If you love me, you will keep my commandments."

John 14:15

CHAPTER 18

Loving Others

You shall love your neighbor as yourself.

Matthew 22:39

Now we will talk about the Commandments which help us to love others as we love ourselves.

Loving Yourself

Before we begin you must not get the idea that when we say you should love others *as* yourself that you should love others *instead* of yourself. God wants you to love yourself. He made your body and your soul, and he loves you much more than you can imagine. He even loved you enough to die for you!

But in a way, you do not need to be told to love yourself because, as a result of Adam's sin, we all tend to love ourselves too much and to love others too little. That is why we need to be told to love others as ourselves, and that is what the next seven Commandments help us to do.

4. Honor your father and your mother.

You and your family are pilgrims to heaven together in a special way because it is your parents who must guide you to heaven. For this reason, the Fourth Commandment is a very im-portant one for you. Also, the more you **honor** your parents, the happier your family will be. What this Commandment means by honor is to *love*, to *respect*, and to *obey* your parents.

Loving Your Parents

Because your parents loved each other, they cooperated with God's grace to give you life. And they continue to love you by trying to do what is best for you. Think of some of the things that your parents have done for you— whether big or little—things like taking care of you when you were sick, feeding you every day, providing your clothes, helping you with your homework, or celebrating your birthday.

No one really has to tell you to love your parents in return—you already do—but your love needs to grow and to be shown in the right ways. Most of all, loving your parents means caring about them, being thankful to them, and wanting good things for them, especially for them to go to heaven. If you love your parents, you will pray for them. You will also try to be of help to them and never hurt or disappoint them. And you will always tell them the truth. Can you think of some little ways to let them know that you love them—such as by telling them so,

by planning a surprise for them, by doing things for them? When they are old or sick you can then return what they have given you by taking care of them.

Respecting Your Parents

How do you treat people you respect? First of all, you are careful about their feelings and wishes because you think so highly of them. Also, you are polite to them; you are never rude. You say "please" and "thank you" when you ask for things. In order to please God you must treat your mother and father in this way.

Obeying Your Parents

Does your mother have to ask you again and again to clean your room or to do the dishes? Often it is hard to obey at once because you are asked to do something just when you are going out to play or are watching a show. It will help if you think of how much it will

please your mother if you obey her cheerfully and quickly.

Sometimes you must obey your parents when they tell you that you cannot do something that you want very much to do. Being good is not always easy, but one thing that might make it easier to obey is to remember that your parents love you and want what is best for you. When they forbid you to do something, it is because they care about you.

Time Away from Home

Your life at home with your family is not the only part of your life. You should also honor priests, especially your parish priests. You call them "Father." You should respect and obey those in authority in the Church.

Your parents have given your teachers permission to guide you while you are at school. Because of this, you should respect and obey your teachers.

Anyone else who takes the place of your

parents for a while should be honored. Baby-sitters and your friends' parents are some examples of these.

5. *You shall not kill.*

Maybe you are thinking, "I don't have to be concerned about the Fifth Commandment because I will never kill anyone." But through this Commandment, God is letting us know that there are other ways of hurting someone's life besides killing him.

We have two lives—the life of our bodies and the life of God in our souls. In the Fifth Commandment, God tells us to respect both lives in ourselves and in others.

Taking Care of
Your Body . . .

Think of what a wonderful thing your body is! It has eyes that see and ears that hear sounds. It has a brain with which you think. God made your body, and he will raise it from the dead and bring it to heaven at the end of the world. He expects you to take care of it by giving it the right amount of exercise, food, and sleep.

Above all, make up your mind right now to stay away from all illegal drugs and other dangers because they can kill you. Since our bodies and souls are so closely connected, when something is wrong with our bodies, it can often have a bad effect on our souls.

. . . And the
Bodies of Others

Do you ever get so angry with your brother, sister, or friend that finally you hit the person? Or have you ever teased someone who was weaker than you or shoved him? If so, these things are signs that you are not respecting other people's bodies as you do your own.

Taking Care
Of Your Soul . . .

The Fifth Commandment also tells you to take care of the life of grace in your soul. Of your two lives, this is really the more important one because your soul is the higher part of you. You take care of your soul by praying, receiving the sacraments, and doing good deeds.

. . . And the
Souls of Others

Do you remember what Cain said when God asked him where Abel was: "Am I my brother's keeper?" The answer to that question is "yes;" we are our brothers' and sisters' keepers! That means that we are not going to heaven alone but we are here to help other people love God and each other. Because of this, you must be careful not to harm the precious souls of your family, friends, and acquaintances.

How can you avoid harming someone else's soul? First of all, you must try not to set a bad example which would lead him to sin. For if he sees you do bad things, he might think that it is all right for him to do them too. This is called giving **scandal** to someone.

We should also not be unkind to others because that is a way of hurting their souls, and it might even lead them to sin. Is there someone you won't play with because he is unattractive or foolish? Or is there someone you make fun of because he is not good at baseball or basketball? Do you talk about others and harm their reputations?

Wishing Others Harm

Not only must we be careful not to hurt others, but we must not even *wish* that they were hurt. Have you ever been so angry at someone that you wished that he would get into trouble? Have you ever been happy that someone was hurt or punished? This is also against the Fifth Commandment.

Loving Your Enemies

How many times have you said of someone at school or your brother or sister, "I hate him," or "I hate her?" Well, of course you didn't really mean that you hate the person because hate is a very terrible thing. It makes people's souls wither and die. What you meant was that the person made you very angry or very afraid or that he hurt you.

But Jesus wants you to make a special effort to forgive those who have hurt you, to love those who seem disagreeable, or who are not easy to get along with. You should ask Jesus for help in doing this. You should never stop speaking to someone or refuse to be friends again because you are mad at him. If someone refuses to be your friend, you can pray for him and hope that some day you will be friends again.

Now that you know the Fourth and the Fifth Commandments, you should try to be someone who loves, respects, and obeys his parents and those in authority (Fourth); and respects his own body and soul as well as those of others (Fifth).

Words to Know:

honor   scandal

"Children, obey your parents in everything, for this pleases the Lord."

Colossians 3:20

Q. 69   *What does the Fourth Commandment tell us to do?*
The Fourth Commandment orders us to love, respect, and obey our parents and whoever holds authority over us (CCC 2199).

Q. 70   *What are we told to do by the Fifth Commandment?*
The Fifth Commandment orders us to be of good will to all, including our enemies, and to respect our bodies and souls as well as those of our neighbors. We must do all we can to protect life from its very beginning to natural death (CCC 2258, 2319).

Q. 71   *What does the Fifth Commandment forbid?*
The Fifth Commandment forbids us to harm the lives of our neighbors or ourselves. It forbids murder, suicide, fighting (out of anger), curses, and scandal (CCC 2261, 2262, 2270, 2284).

CHAPTER 19

Growing in Love

A new commandment I give to you, that you love one another; even as I have loved you, that you also love one another.

John 13:34

6. *You shall not commit adultery.*

9. *You shall not covet your neighbor's wife.*

Loving Good Things

The Sixth and Ninth Commandments are laws that protect marriages and families. They help to make children's homes happy and secure places in which to grow up. These laws forbid unfaithfulness in marriage. But they have a message for you too. God tells you through these Commandments to enjoy only good books, magazines, movies, TV shows, and jokes and to stay away from impure things that would stop you from having the beautiful soul that God wants you to have. Here is a good way to tell if a joke, a book, a movie, or a TV show is not pleasing to God: would you be embarrassed to tell your parents or your teacher about it? Is it something that has to be whispered about? If it is, then you probably should stay away from it. Fill your mind with every-

thing that is good and pure. Remember your body is called to be a temple of the Holy Spirit, so guard your thoughts and actions and keep them pure and pleasing to God.

7. *You shall not steal.*

10. *You shall not covet your neighbor's goods.*

Stealing

Although everything, including ourselves, really belongs to God, he lets us own things for the time that we are on earth. To take what belongs to someone else is against the Seventh Commandment. It is wrong to go into a store and steal something. Although most of us would not do this, there are other ways of stealing that we must avoid. Taking things in school or at home that belong to others is stealing. Cheating on a test is a way of stealing someone else's knowledge. Also, borrowing something and not returning it is the same as stealing it.

Damaging Private Property

Even if you do not take what belongs to others, you must be careful not to damage it. If you borrow something, it should be returned in the same condition as when you received it. If you are playing near a neighbor's property, you should be careful not to damage it.

Being Content

The Tenth Commandment is like the Seventh because they both are about things that don't belong to us. But whereas the Seventh tells us not to take what is not ours, the Tenth tells us not even to **covet** it, which means to want it more than we should. There is nothing wrong with wanting things, but often we want them too much or for the wrong reasons. For example, sometimes we want whatever someone else has. Sometimes we feel **envy**, which means that when someone else gets something nice or receives a compliment, instead of being happy for him, we are sad because we feel that such good things should come to us.

The Tenth Commandment also tells us to be patient, which means that we must wait calmly for the things we want and that we should not get upset if we don't get them. We should also try to be patient when things don't go our own way, because we know that God permits suffering in every life to make us better than we are.

8. *You shall not bear false witness against your neighbor.*

Loving the Truth

Once Jesus called the devil "the father of lies." This was because the very first lie came from the devil. As you remember, he told Eve that the fruit from the Tree of the Knowledge of Good and Evil would not cause her to die. The Eighth Commandment, "You shall not bear **false witness** against your neighbor," tells us not to follow the devil's example by lying, and it also tells us to love the **truth**.

Do you know what truth is? When something is true, it really *is*. When we love the truth, we see and talk about things as they really are. This means that we will always try to look for and tell the truth even when it is hard to do so.

Sometimes we might lie because we are afraid of getting into trouble. This happens when we have already done something wrong, and we are afraid of being punished. There is a cure for this. The more we follow the other Commandments and avoid doing wrong, the less we will feel the need to lie. Then we will be much happier and more peaceful.

At other times we might lie because we want to feel important. Then we tell our friends stories about ourselves or our parents that are not true. Any time we need to feel important, we should remember that we *are* important, because Jesus loves us.

Even if we don't quite lie when we talk to our friends, we must be careful not even to exaggerate. When we exaggerate, we start out with something true but we build it up so much with things that are not true that it ends up being a lie.

And then there are the lies of **flattery**. Flattery is saying something nice (but maybe even untrue) about someone just because we hope he will like us or do something for us.

The worst kind of lie to tell is a lie to get someone in trouble. This kind of lie is not only untrue but also very unkind and mean.

If we love the truth, we will also try not to jump to conclusions before we know what really happened. Sometimes we are quick to blame others for something only to discover later that they were not at fault.

But even when we love the truth, we need not always tell *all* that is true. Sometimes something

> "... whatever is true, whatever is honorable, whatever is just, whatever is pure, whatever is lovely, whatever is gracious, if there is any excellence, if there is anything worthy of praise, think about these things."
>
> Philippians 4:8

is true but it would hurt another person's feelings, so it is better not to say it. Or sometimes a friend might tell you something private that he does not want anyone else to know. Some people like to **gossip**. When we gossip, we talk about true things but they are things about other people which are private, and they are often things that others don't have a right to know.

Repairing the Damage Done

There is a story about a man who stole one hundred dollars from his neighbor. After he had spent the money, God touched his heart, and he was very sorry. He then confessed his crime to his neighbor.

"I'm glad you're sorry," replied the neighbor, "and I forgive you with all my heart. But what shall we do about the money you stole? I need it to buy food for my family."

"I'll work until I earn it and then I will pay you back," said the repentant thief.

In much the same way, if we have injured someone, whether by stealing from him, damaging his property, hurting his body or his soul, or lying about him, God is pleased that we are sorry, but we must still repair the damage we have done as much as we can. If we make an honest effort to do this, God will be pleased. If you have hurt someone, you should apologize, and if you have lied about someone, you should confess your lie to the person you told it to.

From what you have learned fro[m] and Ninth, Seventh and Tenth, Commandments, you should try to be one who stays away from bad books, jokes, movies, and TV shows (Sixth and Ninth), respects private property and does not even covet it (Seventh and Tenth), and loves the truth (Eighth).

Joyful Goodness

If you feel as if you have just read so many "do's" and "don'ts" about the Commandments and you are beginning to think that there is no joy in being a Christian, that is the exact opposite of the truth!

The truth is that obeying the Commandments is the only way you will be really happy in this life and in the next. Disobeying them (besides being wrong) leads to unhappiness, as we saw with Adam and Eve. Tricked by the devil they thought they would be happy. But they became as unhappy as anyone could be.

Being really and truly good makes you joyful and the kind of person others want for a friend. And the better you become, the more God's love will shine out from you so that your family and friends can see it.

Imagine a person who would keep the Commandments just the way they should be kept. That person would love God and others very much. He would always tell the truth, which means that people would believe and trust him. He would never make fun of you or be mean. He would never want to hurt you. You would want such a person to be your best friend. He would be the most wonderful person you could know.

Words to Know:

covet envy truth
false witness flattery gossip

Q. 72 *What does the Sixth Commandment forbid?*

The Sixth Commandment forbids impurity of any kind. It forbids immoral acts, words, books, pictures, movies, and shows (CCC 2525, 2336).

Q. 73 *What does the Ninth Commandment forbid?*

The Ninth Commandment forbids bad thoughts and desires (CCC 2514, 2517).

Q. 74 *What does the Seventh Commandment tell us to do?*

The Seventh Commandment tells us to respect other people's property, to repair damages that we cause, and to honor our debts (CCC 2411–12).

Q. 75 *What does the Seventh Commandment forbid?*

The Seventh Commandment forbids damaging our neighbor's property and stealing from our neighbors (CCC 2401).

Q. 76 *What does the Tenth Commandment tell us to do?*

The Tenth Commandment tells us to be just and moderate in the desire to improve our own condition in life, and to suffer with patience the hardships and other sufferings permitted by the Lord for our merit (CCC 2538, 2545, 2549).

Q. 77 *What does the Tenth Commandment forbid?*

The Tenth Commandment forbids an unhealthy desire for riches that disregards the rights and welfare of our neighbors (CCC 2536).

Q. 78 *What does the Eighth Commandment tell us to do?*

The Eighth Commandment tells us to speak the truth carefully and to interpret in the best possible way the actions of our neighbor (CCC 2468, 2478).

Q. 79 *What does the Eighth Commandment forbid?*

The Eighth Commandment forbids lying and damaging another's reputation. This includes false witness, flattery, unfounded suspicion, and rash judgment (CCC 2464, 2477).

Q. 80 *If one has unjustly harmed another's reputation, is he obliged to repair the damage done?*

If one damages another's reputation through false accusations, wicked talk about him, or even by speaking an unnecessary truth, he must do everything in his power to repair the damage done (CCC 2487).

"For this is the love of God, that we keep his commandments."

1 John 5:3

CHAPTER 20

Jesus, Our Guide

When the centurion and those who were with him, keeping watch over Jesus, saw the earthquake and what took place, they were filled with awe, and said, "Truly this was the Son of God!"

Matthew 27:54

I AM

Wherever Jesus, the new king of Israel, went, he was followed about angry men who argued with him because they did not like what he was saying or doing. Some of these men were **Pharisees**. Some of the Pharisees were so concerned with the special laws that God had given them through Moses that they often forgot about loving God and others. Instead, they thought only of themselves. They thought they were perfect, and they wanted to look perfect by following every law without making one little mistake. But their hearts were cold, proud, and unloving. The things that Jesus said and the way he lived made them look less good and so they were against him. They often asked him trick questions.

One day the Pharisees were very annoyed because Jesus had said, "If anyone keeps my word, he will never die." Of course, Jesus was talking about living forever in heaven, but the Pharisees did not even try to understand that.

"Surely you do not pretend to be greater than our father Abraham and the prophets, and *they* died. Just who do you claim to be?" they asked.

"Your father Abraham was glad to see my day," Jesus replied.

"You are not even fifty years old but you claim to have seen Abraham?" they shouted.

"Before Abraham was," Jesus replied, "I AM." With these words, Jesus was telling them that he is the same God who talked to Moses and gave his name as "Yahweh" or "I AM." But this was very hard for the Jews to accept because they knew that the God of Abraham, Isaac, and Moses was pure spirit with no body, and here was a man who claimed to be that God.

But Jesus was both God and man! As a child, Jesus began to grow, through the power of the Holy Spirit, in the womb of his mother, Mary. From the first moment of his humanity, he had a body and soul like ours, but his body and soul were joined to God in such a way that they were not two **persons** but only one! Jesus is one Divine Person, truly God and truly man.

The way we try to understand this is to say that Jesus is one *Divine Person* with *two* **natures**. An angel is a person and you are a person. How many persons are in your class or family?

When we talk about *nature*, we mean what a thing is. What are you? You are a human being. What is Gabriel? Gabriel is an angel. What is the earth? The earth is a planet.

For all these things the answer to the question, "What is it?," will be simple, but Jesus is the exception. If you asked Jesus, "What are you?" he could answer, "I am a human being," *but* he could also answer, "I am God."

Do you find all this hard to understand? That is not surprising because only God really understands it. This is a **mystery**. A mystery is something that our human minds cannot completely understand. It is God who told (or revealed) it to us, and, even after he has revealed it to us we still don't really understand it. It is not *against* our reason but it is *beyond* our reason.

The Worker of Miracles

Jesus' teachings were so new and wonderful that when some people heard him they remarked, "No man has ever spoken like this man!"

Jesus wanted the people of Israel to accept his teachings and to believe that he is God, the Son of God who was to be the Savior, so that he could heal them of their sins and give them eternal life. Once, Jesus even wept over the city of Jerusalem because he cared so much. He had tried so many times to get its people to accept God's mercy in sending them his beloved Son, but they would not accept it. And this was after he had done many **miracles** to show them who he was!

A miracle is an act above the laws of nature that only God can perform. Sometimes God performs a miracle to prove that a person he has sent is telling the truth.

Moses proved to Pharaoh that it was God's message to let the people of Israel go into the desert. God worked many miracles to show that Moses was sent by him. In our own time, when Mary, Christ's mother, has appeared on earth, those who have not seen her have often asked for a sign. Through her, God has cured sick people and done many other wonders, like making summer flowers bloom in winter, as a sign that she really has been sent by God, as in the appearance of Our Lady of Guadalupe.

Jesus too worked many, many miracles as signs of his divinity. But Jesus' signs showed that not only was he sent from God but that he *is* God. Everyone else had worked miracles by asking God for the power. But since Jesus was God, he worked them by his *own* power.

Here are some of the miracles Jesus worked. He made blind people see, deaf people hear, and dumb people speak. He also cured people of all kinds of sicknesses, and he even brought dead people back to life!

He was able to calm the sea and make the wind stop. Jesus also showed that he was God by the control he had over the fallen angels who were seeking to harm God's children. Jesus commanded them to leave and they went away at once. This made people remark, "Who is this? With authority he commands even unclean spirits and they obey him!"

The Only Way To Heaven

Jesus is the great God, full of majesty and power. However, when he became man he came very close to you. He loves you tenderly, and you can speak to him even more freely and trustfully than you could to your best friend. You know that a best friend will always be looking out for the things that are going to make you happy. This is someone who is always ready to listen and who loves to be with you. In fact, Jesus is *more* wonderful than a best friend could ever be. The joy that Jesus will give you no one can ever take away!

Jesus is waiting for you now on earth and then in heaven, where he will satisfy your every hope. And only by following him can you be with him. Every single person who is in heaven right now got there only by following Jesus. Even the people in heaven who did not know

> ". . . it is no longer I who live, but Christ who lives in me."
>
> Galatians 2:20

about Jesus while they were on earth really had followed him without knowing it!

Here are some things that you can do to grow closer to and follow your friend Jesus: 1) receive him often in Holy Communion so that he can live in you; 2) talk to him every day; 3) follow him by keeping the Commandments and by helping others as much as you can.

> Christ be with me, Christ within me,
> Christ behind me, Christ before me,
> Christ beside me, Christ to win me,
> Christ to comfort and restore me,
> Christ beneath me, Christ above me,
> Christ in quiet, Christ in danger,
> Christ in hearts of all that love me,
> Christ in mouth of friend and
>   stranger. . . .
>
> St. Patrick's Breastplate

Words to Know:

Pharisees   person
nature   mystery   miracle

"I am the way, and the truth, and the life; no one comes to the Father, but by me."

John 14:6

Q. 81   *Is Jesus Christ God and man?*

Yes, Jesus Christ is true God and true man (CCC 469).

Q. 82   *How did the Son of God become man?*

The Son of God became man by taking a human body and soul in the pure womb of the Virgin Mary, by the work of the Holy Spirit. This is called the Incarnation (CCC 484–85).

Q. 83   *Did the Son of God cease to be God when he became man?*

No, when the Son of God became man, he did not cease to be God, but remained fully God while at the same time becoming fully man (CCC 464, 470).

Q. 84   *Are there two natures in Jesus Christ?*

Yes, there are two natures in Jesus Christ: divine nature and human nature (CCC 464–70).

Q. 85   *With the two natures in Jesus Christ, are there also two persons?*

With the two natures in Jesus Christ, there are not two persons, but only one: the Divine Person of the Son of God (CCC 468).

Q. 86   *What is a mystery?*

A mystery is a truth beyond our reason, but not contrary to it, revealed by God (CCC 42).

Q. 87   *What is a miracle?*

A miracle is a sign, which is beyond the laws of nature, and therefore something that can be worked only by God (CCC 548).

Q. 88   *With what miracles did Jesus Christ confirm his teachings and show that he is true God?*

Jesus Christ confirmed his teaching and showed that he is true God by restoring vision to the blind, hearing to the deaf, speech to the dumb, health to the sick, and life to the dead. He also commanded demons and the forces of nature (CCC 515, 548).

CHAPTER 21

"For This I Have Come Into the World"

For as in Adam all die, so also in Christ shall all be made alive.

1 Corinthians 15:22

The Gift of God's Mercy

People sometimes ask, "Since God knows everything, did he not know that Adam and Eve would sin? If he did know, why did he create them in the first place?"

The answer to that question is that God *did* know that Adam and Eve would sin. But he created them out of love, and he gave them free will so that they could choose to love him. He did not want to force them to be his friends, although to be his friends meant happiness and bliss for them.

Sin and evil are certainly against the will of God. Still, everything that has ever happened or ever will happen will finally be worked out for the good at the end of the world. Christ will be victorious over evil. You are part of God's plan—we all are. But as to why God does things as he does, that is not up to us to understand fully. That is beyond us.

Of course, to sin is the most horrible thing we can do, and the sin of Adam was terrible. It brought all the suffering into the world. Still, God is so great that he could make something

good out of it all in the end. As a result of Adam's sin, God sent us a Redeemer, his only Son. This was an undeserved gift of his mercy. He created us out of love and he then redeemed us out of love. To **redeem** means to free someone from slavery by buying freedom for him. The fact that God *did* become one of us is a great honor to poor creatures made out of the dust of the earth. Even the angels were not honored in this way. God never became an angel, but he did become a man!

To see how God's becoming man could be such an honor for the human race, it might help to think of a family. In a family, when one member becomes president or famous in some way, the whole family is honored. How much more are we honored that God's only Son has become a member of our human family!

Jesus Suffers and Dies

But you must not think that because God planned to become a man and save us, it was

easy for Jesus to suffer and to die for us. Jesus Christ as God could not suffer or die, because God is unchangeable, but Jesus as man suffered extreme agony. Just as Joseph in the Old Testament was betrayed by his brothers, Jesus was betrayed by one of his friends and apostles. He sweated blood on the night before his death. Finally, he suffered from very painful scourging and died by being crucified, having his hands and feet nailed to a wooden cross. He did this out of love, knowing it was his Father's will for our salvation and that God would bring good out of the evil of his death—the gates of heaven would be opened.

This is the new Passover. When the Jews were in slavery in Egypt and the tenth plague came, Moses told the Jewish people to sprinkle their doorposts with the blood of the lamb to protect them, so that the angel of death would *pass over* them. After eating the lamb (the Passover meal) they would be delivered. In a similar way, the Blood of Jesus, the Lamb of God, has delivered us from the slavery of sin and from the eternal pains of hell. When we receive the Blood of the Lamb of God in Holy Communion, Jesus shares his life with us and strengthens our souls.

Descent into Hell

Since his death opened the gates of heaven, Christ went to lift up all the souls of the good people who had died before his time and bring them to heaven. Think of the souls that probably were there: Adam, Eve, Abraham, Moses, Samuel, and Jesus' foster father, Joseph. Think of the joy there must have been, because they had all been waiting for that moment for so long!

The Resurrection

"Destroy this temple," said Jesus, "and in three days I will raise it up." The people knew all the work that had gone into restoring Solomon's temple after it had been destroyed by the Babylonians and then rebuilt twice, the last time by King Herod.

"It has taken forty-six years to build this temple, and you will raise it up in three days?" they asked angrily. But Jesus was speaking not of Solomon's temple, but of the temple of his body. Because he was God, his body was God's temple in a special way. And so, on the third day after he died, the most wonderful and incredible thing happened—Jesus *did* raise up the temple! He took up the temple of his body, which had been buried and came back to a new life.

The Ascension

Jesus' mission was accomplished. And it was time for him to return to his Father. But before he left for good, he appeared many times to his disciples to show them that he really *had* risen from the dead. Because he had been killed, his poor, frightened friends at first thought that they had been wrong in believing he was the one who would save the people of Israel. When Jesus rose, they could not believe it and they thought that they were seeing a ghost! However, by eating and drinking with them and letting them touch him, Jesus showed them he was really alive again.

Once Jesus had risen from the dead, the disciples began to understand more and more that Jesus came to save the children of Israel and all of God's children by giving them eternal life. He would one day raise up their bodies to live forever in heaven. That was so much better than restoring the earthly kingdom of the Israelites. Now that they understood this, Jesus could explain his teaching to them in more detail.

Forty days after his Resurrection, Jesus ascended to heaven, alive and exactly as he was on that first Easter Sunday with his body—but he did not really leave them. He told them that he would be with them always and he was—and still is! He sent them the Holy Spirit.

As God, Jesus is everywhere. As God and man he is watching over you right now from heaven just as he is watching over everyone. But he was not content just to stay in heaven—he wanted to be near us so much that the same Jesus who rose on Easter Sunday is hidden under the appearances of bread and wine in the Eucharist.

Words to Know:

redeem   Descent into Hell
Resurrection   Ascension

Rejoice, O earth, in shining splendor,
Radiant in the brightness of your King:
Christ has conquered! Glory fills you!
Darkness vanishes for ever!
This is our Passover feast,
When Christ, the true Lamb, is slain,
Whose blood consecrates the homes of all believers.
This is the night when first you saved our fathers:
You freed the people of Israel from their slavery
And led them dry-shod through the sea.
This is the night when Jesus Christ
Broke the chains of death
And rose triumphant from the grave.
What good would life have been to us,
Had not Christ come as our Redeemer?
O happy fault, O necessary sin of Adam,
Which gained for us so great a Redeemer!
The power of this holy night
Dispels all evil, washes guilt away,
Restores lost innocence, brings mourners joy.
Night truly blessed when heaven is wedded to earth
And man is reconciled with God.

Exsultet—Easter Vigil hymn

"Jesus Christ is the same yesterday and today and for ever."

Hebrews 13:8

Q. 89 *Why did the Son of God become man?*

The Son of God became man to save us from sin and to regain heaven for us (CCC 456–60).

Q. 90 *What did Jesus Christ do to save us?*

To save us, Jesus Christ offered himself as the perfect Sacrifice to the Father by his death on the Cross, and he taught us how to live according to God's will (CCC 461, 462, 571).

Q. 91 *What did Jesus do between his death and Resurrection?*

After his death on Good Friday Jesus descended into hell to take the souls of the just with him into heaven. Then he rose again from the dead on Easter Sunday, taking up his body, which had been buried (CCC 632–35, 638).

Q. 92 *How long did the body of Jesus Christ remain buried?*

The body of Jesus Christ remained buried from Friday evening to Easter Sunday morning (CCC 627).

Q. 93 *What did Jesus Christ do after his Resurrection?*

After his Resurrection, Jesus Christ remained on earth forty days and taught his apostles all they needed to know to continue his ministry through the Church he had founded. Then he ascended to heaven, where he sits at the right hand of God the Father almighty (CCC 642, 659).

Q. 94 *Why did Jesus Christ remain on earth forty days after his Resurrection?*

Jesus Christ remained on earth forty days after his Resurrection in order to show that he had really and truly risen from the dead, to confirm his disciples in their faith in him, and to instruct them more profoundly in his teaching (CCC 642).

Q. 95 *At the present time is Jesus Christ only in heaven?*

At the present time, Jesus Christ is not only in heaven, but as God he is everywhere, by the Holy Spirit he is within his Church, and as God-man he is also in the world in the Holy Eucharist (CCC 663, 667–69).

CHAPTER 22

The Perfect Sacrifice

And by that will we have been sanctified through the offering of the body of Jesus Christ once for all. . . . For by a single offering he has perfected for all time those who are sanctified.

Hebrews 10:10, 14

Sacrifices

"My bike," "my dog," "my toys," "my room" —from the time we are little, we own things. Often one of the things very young children learn to say is "mine." That is all right because God has allowed us to own things. Because of the effects of original sin in us, however, we sometimes may forget who really owns things and who gave them to us. We can become selfish.

Abel, Noah, Abraham, Isaac, Jacob, and many others never wanted to forget that all that they owned really belonged to God and that he was just letting them use these things for the time they were on earth. They also wanted to adore him, to thank him for his gifts, and to ask for his blessings in the future. And when they sinned, they wanted God to know that they were sorry for having offended him. They wanted to atone for (make up for) their sins. So they took their best animals or their best crops—things that would have been good to eat or could have been sold for a lot of money— and they offered them up to God. By burning them, they destroyed them and, in this way, gave them back to God.

Later in their history the people of Israel still offered **sacrifices** to God. But now, instead of offering the sacrifices themselves, they would go to the temple and give the best of what they had or could afford to a priest who would offer it up for them. Do you remember which tribe it was that God appointed to be the priests and offer sacrifices for the people of Israel? It was the tribe of Levi.

There were two kinds of sacrifice. The first was of something which did not have blood— like ears of corn, oil, and flour. And then there were the sacrifices which involved blood—animal sacrifices.

Sin Offerings

Every time a sacrifice was made for sins, it had to be an animal sacrifice. Animals were the people's prize possessions. It was the best thing they could give to God to atone for sins.

The priest would put his hands on the animal's head as a sign that he would like to transfer the man's sins onto the animal. And then, after the animal **victim** was killed, the priest would drain its blood and sprinkle it on the altar. The sprinkling of the blood was the important part of the sacrifice because blood was, and still is, thought of as the life of the body. When the blood was sprinkled, it was clear that the life of the animal was being given to atone for sins.

Mission from the Father

When Jesus was a child, the Jews were still offering sacrifices. Once when he was twelve, Jesus and his parents were in Jerusalem for the feast of Passover. He slipped away and went to the temple to do some special work that his Father had given him to do. He must have seen the animals being killed so that they could be offered to his Father. Jesus had a special mis-sion from that same Father. He would grow up and offer to the Father a life of perfect obedi-ence leading to the perfect sacrifice of himself on the Cross.

The Perfect Sacrifice

Jesus Christ's sacrifice was perfect in every way: 1) Since Adam had sinned, and all mankind in him, the sacrifice needed to be one which involved blood, to atone for our sins. The sprinkling or the shedding of the blood was the most important part of the sacrifice; therefore, Christ's blood was shed for us on the Cross. 2) The lamb or other animal victim had to be the best of the flock. Jesus is called the "spotless lamb" because he is not only sinless and per-fect, but he is also God himself. 3) Although it was just a symbol when the priest put his hands on the animal's head to transfer the man's sins onto it, Jesus *really* took our sins on himself and died for us.

Jesus the Priest

Jesus Christ was not only the Sacrifice itself. He was also the one who offered the sacrifice. Because he is God, in a second Jesus could have stopped the men who were killing him! But he freely offered himself as a victim for us. Because Jesus is the one who offered the Sacrifice, he is also a priest. Jesus is the greatest priest who offered up the greatest Sacrifice ever.

The Mass

That Sacrifice is still going on, although the Crucifixion took place once and for all on a hill called Calvary about two thousand years ago. Each time Holy **Mass** is celebrated, Jesus becomes really and truly present on the altar and offers himself up—his Body and Blood—for our sins, as a renewal of and in remembrance of the Sacrifice on Calvary and in memory of his death and Resurrection. The temple in Jerusalem has been replaced by Catholic churches everywhere and the altar in the temple and the Cross of Christ has been replaced by the altar in your church!

The Liturgy of the Mass

When the priest offered a sacrifice before the Ark of the Covenant, there were special prayers and ceremonies to go with it.

In the same way, although Christ's Sacrifice is complete when the priest says, "This is my Body" and "This is my Blood" over the bread and wine, we have prayers and ceremonies that go with this Sacrifice. These prayers and cere-

monies with the Sacrifice are called the Liturgy of the Mass. They are very important and everyone in the Church takes part in them in certain ways.

Liturgy of the Word

The Mass is divided into two main parts. In the first part, the **Liturgy of the Word**, we listen as someone reads from the word of God, the Bible. Since the Holy Spirit inspired the writers of the Bible to tell us what he wants us to know, the message that comes from it is God himself speaking to us. On Sundays, we hear three readings. Two of them are from the Old Testament, the Acts of the Apostles, the New Testament Epistles, or Revelation. The third one comes from one of the four **Gospels**, which are accounts of the life of Jesus.

Also on Sundays the priest will explain the word of God to us. This is called the **homily**. The priest is trying to help us understand the message from God that we have just heard in the readings.

Liturgy of the Eucharist

Then comes the second part of the Mass: the **Liturgy of the Eucharist**. This is when the actual Sacrifice takes place. There are prayers for the living and the dead and prayers of offering, atonement for sins, praise, adoration, and thanksgiving. This is also when we receive Holy Communion, Jesus, our sacred Food, who will help us to put into practice the words of the Bible we have just heard. He will also increase the life of grace in our souls.

"Look with favor on your Church's offering, and see the victim whose death has reconciled us to yourself. . . ."

Third Eucharistic Prayer

Finally, the priest tells us to "go in peace." The word Mass comes from the Latin word *missio*, a form of *mittere*, which means "to send." When the Mass is over, God, through the priest, sends you home with his grace to bring Christ's love to others and to love and serve him.

We Must Participate at Mass

Think of how great the Mass is! Each Mass is a renewal of Christ's Sacrifice on the Cross in memory of his death and Resurrection. It is the most important thing that ever happened in the whole history of the world. It is the greatest act of worship that we can give to God. Because of this, you are required to participate at Mass at least on Sundays and Holy Days of Obligation. This means we must listen to the word of God and offer our prayers and our very selves to God during the Mass. We are also obliged to receive Holy Communion once a year during the Easter Season.

Words to Know:

sacrifice   victim   Mass
Liturgy of the Word   Gospel   homily
Liturgy of the Eucharist

Q. 96   ***What is the Holy Mass?***
The Holy Mass is the Sacrifice of the Body and Blood of Jesus Christ, which is offered by the priest to God, under the appearances of bread and wine, in remembrance of the Sacrifice of the Cross (CCC 1341–46).

Q. 97   ***What is a sacrifice?***
A sacrifice is a public offering to God of a thing which is destroyed to give it back to God (CCC 1357).

Q. 98   ***Is the Sacrifice of the Mass the same as the Sacrifice of the Cross?***
The Sacrifice of the Mass is the same sacrifice as the Sacrifice of the Cross, the only difference is in the way it is offered (CCC 1364).

Q. 99   ***What is the difference between the Sacrifice of the Cross and the Sacrifice of the Mass?***
On the Cross, Jesus Christ offered himself in a bloody manner; on the altar, Jesus Christ offers himself sacramentally, in an unbloody manner, by the ministry of the priest (CCC 1366–67).

Q. 100   ***Are we obliged to take part in Mass?***
We are obliged to take part in Mass on Sunday and on the Holy Days of Obligation. It is good also to attend Mass frequently, in order to participate in the greatest act of religion, the one that is most pleasing to God, and best for us (CCC 2176).

CHAPTER 23

Bread from Heaven

I am the living bread which came down from heaven; if any one eats of this bread, he will live for ever; and the bread which I shall give for the life of the world is my flesh.

John 6:51

Bread in the Desert

You remember when the children of Israel were in the desert and did not have enough food. They complained to Moses that it was impossible for them to continue their pilgrim journey to the Promised Land because they were hungry and too weak. Then God heard their prayers and had pity on them. In his great mercy he would send them food. "I will rain down bread from heaven for you," he said to Moses.

The next morning they found the ground covered with a delicate and flaky white substance with a wonderfully sweet taste, like wafers made with honey.

They called it "manna." It gave them strength to continue their journey. The Israelites ate manna for forty years, up until the time they came into the Promised Land.

In order to help you and give you strength for your journey on this earth on your way to heaven (our Promised Land), you too can have Bread from heaven. And the Bread that you can receive is much, much better than manna because if you eat it you will have everlasting life!

You might be wondering where to get such wonderful Bread. You receive this **Living Bread** every time you go to Holy Communion!

But how can bread be "living" or alive? This Bread is not really bread. It looks and tastes like bread, but it is really Jesus hidden under the appearances of bread. How can such a thing be? Here is how it all began.

The day after Jesus had miraculously multiplied five loaves of bread for a multitude of five thousand, some of these people were secretly hoping that he would do the same thing again. Jesus could tell that this was what they wanted. He wanted them to see that there were much more important things than the food which feeds only the body. He was going to give them something to feed their souls. "My Father gives you true Bread from heaven," he said. "I am the *Living Bread* which comes down from heaven. If anyone eats of this Bread, he will live forever. And the Bread which I give for the life of the world is my Flesh." But as yet, Jesus had not given the people this Bread.

The Last Supper

At Christ's last celebration of the feast of Passover before he died he gave us this Living Bread. It was a Thursday evening, and he and his twelve apostles were eating the lamb, the bitter herbs, and the unleavened bread—the customary Jewish Passover meal. Jesus had told them he was going to die soon and that one of them was going to betray him.

Jesus loved them so much. Because he was about to leave them, he wanted a way of remaining with them. He took some of the unleavened bread that was on the table. He said a blessing over it and then he broke it and gave it to his apostles. "Take this, and eat; this is my Body," he said. After that, he took a cup of wine and passed it to them saying, "Take this, all of you and drink from it, for this is the cup of my Blood of the new covenant which is poured out for many for the forgiveness of sins." And then Jesus told the apostles to do what he had done in remembrance of him. From then on, every time they repeated Jesus' words and actions, Jesus was with them again, present in this special way.

Jesus Is with Us Too

Jesus wants to be with us too. Just as he commanded the apostles, he commands our priests to do what he has done. During the Liturgy of the Eucharist, the Mass follows closely what Jesus himself did at the Last Supper. We even use unleavened bread because that is what Jesus used. That is one of the reasons we use the thin wafers called "hosts." Taking first the bread, the priest says the words of Jesus, "THIS IS MY BODY. . . ." At this exact moment, the bread is truly changed into the Body of Jesus. Next, the priest takes the cup of wine and says, "THIS IS THE CUP OF MY BLOOD. . . ." The wine in the cup is now truly Jesus' Blood, which was

shed for the forgiveness of our sins. This part of the Mass is called the **Consecration**.

The next time you go to Mass, pay special attention to the Consecration. The Host that the priest holds up for us to see and adore is not only Jesus' Body or a part of it. It is Jesus, whole and entire, with his Body, Blood, Soul, and Divinity. And the cup that the priest raises is not only the cup of his Blood. It also contains Jesus, whole and entire, with his Body, Blood, Soul, and Divinity.

Notice that the priest breaks the large Host soon after the Our Father is prayed at Mass. When this happens, you might think that Jesus is not in every broken part. But the truth is that the whole Jesus is in even the tiniest piece of Host and in each drop of Blood in the cup. What is more, every time a Mass is offered anywhere in the world the whole Jesus is there in each one of those Hosts!

The Eucharist

The name we give to Jesus under the appearances of bread and wine is the **Eucharist**.

Eucharist means "giving thanks." And that is a very good name because out of everything that we have to be thankful for, the greatest thing is Jesus' presence among us as Living Bread.

A Holy Meal

You already know now that the Mass is a sacrifice, which renews the Sacrifice of Jesus on the Cross. It is important to know that the Mass is *also* a holy banquet or meal. The altar of sacrifice is also the table of the Lord. We eat at a table. Christ gives himself to us as food. Remember the Passover meal of the Jews, which strengthened them to escape from their slavery in Egypt. The Mass is the new Passover meal. Christ, the Living Bread, gives us the strength to break away from sin and become free truly to love God and others on our earthly pilgrimage. Christ's love is poured into our hearts through this heavenly Food, and we are united with all others in the Church. They become our brothers and sisters. We also call the Mass the **Paschal meal**. Paschal is another word for Passover, and refers to the death and Resurrection of Christ.

A Special Closeness

Jesus gives us himself as Living Bread to be *received*. He wants you to receive him in **Holy Communion**. Communion means unity. When you receive Jesus, you share a special closeness with him. You can offer yourself back to him in communion, too.

Have you ever noticed what it is like when you are good friends with someone? You have a lot in common. You are happy to be together. You love many of the same things.

If you become closer to Jesus by being united with him in Holy Communion, you will become good friends. You will have more and

more in common with him as you share with him your sorrows and joys and think about his. You will be happy to be with him just as he is always happy to be with you. You will love him more and more. You will start to love the people he loves—everyone! He will give you much joy, and the joy that he gives you no one can ever take away!

He has given them Bread from heaven, having all sweetness within it.
Benediction verse

Frequent Communion

Since Jesus is our Food on the way to heaven, we must remember how much we need this Food. Some people eat enough food for their bodies to stay alive, but they are not very healthy. They are likely to get sick because they don't have enough vitamins to protect their bodies. In the same way, some people in the Church receive Jesus only once a year at Easter time, because that is the very least we must do. But that is almost a starvation diet! Jesus asks you to receive him often. He invites you to receive him every Sunday. Many people even receive Jesus every day.

In order to receive Jesus worthily, there are three things to remember: 1) our souls must have God's life of grace in them, which means that we must be free of mortal sin which breaks our friendship with God; 2) we must believe that it is Jesus whom we are going to receive; and 3) we must not eat or drink anything (except medicine or water) for one hour before we go to Communion.

The Tabernacle

Just as the Hebrews had their tabernacle as a way of showing God's special presence with them, we have a tabernacle of our own. In *our* **tabernacle**, which is like a little house made of fine materials and which is found in Catholic churches, Jesus in the Eucharist is kept. It is a very sacred place. There may be a veil on the tabernacle, and a lamp is kept burning as a sign that Jesus is present. Even in the quiet hours of the night, when other lights are out and ev[...] still, there is a light burning in Catholi[...] as a sign that Jesus is there, quietly wai[...] to come and see him anytime we want!

Words to Know:

Living Bread   Consecration   Eucharist
Paschal meal   Holy Communion
tabernacle

Q. 101 *What is the Eucharist?*

The Eucharist is the sacrament that contains the Body, Blood, Soul, and Divinity of our Lord Jesus Christ, under the appearances of bread and wine, for the nourishment of men's souls (CCC 1333).

Q. 102 *When did Jesus Christ institute the Eucharist?*

Jesus Christ instituted the Eucharist at the Last Supper, before his Passion. He consecrated and changed bread and wine into his Body and Blood, then distributed it among the apostles, commanding them to do the same thing in his memory (CCC 1337–41).

Q. 103 *Is the same Jesus Christ, who was born on earth of the Virgin Mary, present in the Eucharist?*

Yes, it is the same Jesus Christ who was born on earth of the Virgin Mary who is present in the Holy Eucharist (CCC 1373).

Q. 104 *What is the host before the Consecration?*

Before the Consecration, the host is bread (CCC 1376–77).

Q. 105 *After the Consecration, what is the Host?*

After the Consecration the Host is the true Body, Blood, Soul, and Divinity of our Lord Jesus Christ under the appearance of bread (CCC 1374–75).

Q. 106 *What does the chalice contain before the Consecration?*

Before the Consecration the chalice contains wine with a small amount of water (CCC 1376–77).

Q. 107   *After the Consecration is there anything left of the bread and wine?*

After the Consecration neither bread nor wine is present any longer. Only the appearance of bread and wine remains, without their substance. All that is really present is the Body, Blood, Soul, and Divinity of Jesus Christ (CCC 1374–75).

Q. 108   *Is only the Body of Jesus Christ present under the appearance of bread and only his Blood under the appearance of the wine?*

No, under the appearance of the bread, Jesus Christ is present whole and entire in Body, Blood, Soul, and Divinity; and under the appearance of wine the whole Jesus is present as well (CCC 1374, 1376–77).

Q. 109   *When the Host is broken into parts, is the Body of Jesus Christ broken?*

When the Host is broken into parts, the Body of Jesus Christ is not broken; the Body of our Lord remains whole and entire in each part of the bread (CCC 1377).

Q. 110   *Is Jesus Christ present in all the consecrated Hosts in the world?*

Yes, Jesus Christ is present in all the consecrated Hosts of the world (CCC 1377).

Q. 111   *What things are necessary for the worthy reception of Holy Communion?*

For a worthy reception of Holy Communion, three things are necessary: first, to be in the grace of God; second, to realize and to consider whom we are about to receive; third to observe the Eucharistic fast (CCC 1385–87).

Q. 112   *How do we observe the Eucharistic fast?*

We observe the Eucharistic fast by not eating or drinking anything (except for water or medicine) for one hour before Communion in order to receive Jesus worthily in the Eucharist (CCC 1387, CIC can. 919).

Q. 113   *Is it good and useful to receive Holy Communion frequently?*

It is very good and most useful to receive Holy Communion frequently, even every day, provided it is done worthily (CCC 1389).

CHAPTER 24

Mistakes Along the Way

The Mighty One, God the LORD, speaks and summons the earth from the rising of the sun to its setting.

Psalm 50:1

The Effects of Original Sin

"Do not eat from it. Do not even touch it, for if you do, you shall die." With these words, God told Adam and Eve what would happen if they chose to turn away from him. Poor Adam and Eve thought that they knew better than God but, of course, they did not. When they disobeyed, they became subject to death and they would have to die some day. They also lost grace. The gates of heaven were closed to them.

But Adam and Eve were not the only ones to suffer from their disobedience. Do you know who else did? All of their descendants beginning with Cain, Abel, and Seth, all the way down to everyone who is alive today, including you! Your body, just like the bodies of Adam and Eve, is going to die someday. And you (like everyone except Jesus, who is God, and Mary, through a special gift) came into being in your mother's womb without God's life in your soul.

By Christ's suffering and death, he won back for us God's life of grace. He gave us the Sacrament of Baptism, through which we receive this grace. But even with grace in our souls, there are still the effects (results) of **original sin** in us. There is still something wrong with us, and that is what we are going to read about now. But before we begin, we must talk about your **conscience**.

Your Conscience

From the time you were a baby, you have been learning to distinguish right from wrong. Your parents said, "No!" when you hit your brother or sister. To make sure that you would know what is right, they encouraged you, for example, to share your toys with others. As you grew older, you learned even more ways of being good. Eventually, you learned the Ten Commandments, which are the really big helps in knowing right from wrong.

You have the ability to judge what you must do to avoid **sin** and do good, using the knowledge you have gained about right and wrong. For example, you might want to go to your friend's house after school. Then you remember that your mother said to come home right away. From the Fourth Commandment you have learned that you must obey your mother. Therefore you decide that to go to your friend's house would be wrong. This judgment about how you ought to act or not to act is called your conscience.

up ruling your mind! For example, you might know that you should obey your mother and come straight home after school, but your desire to go to your friend's house might make you act against what you know is right. Or you might know that it is wrong to hit your brother out of anger, but when he teases you, you get so angry that you hit him anyway. Furthermore, sometimes your desires and feelings might be so strong that this even happens when you are trying very hard to be good!

When we choose to do something that we know is against God's laws, we sin. Adam and Eve committed the first sin, and this is one of the reasons that we call it the original sin. All other sins after that first one are called **actual sins**. These are sins that we ourselves commit (do by choice). Ever since Adam and Eve, people travelling on the road to heaven have gotten at least a little lost by committing sins.

Sin

Now we will see how, as a result of Adam's sin, you are a little mixed up and upside down! Sometimes, although you know what you *should* do, your desire for things and your feelings are out of order. So even though you know you should listen to your conscience, by which you judge that something you want to do is wrong, you sometimes do it anyway. Your mind should rule your desires and your feelings, but sometimes your desires and your feelings end

Mortal Sin

It is possible for a person to get lost in a big way. This happens when he breaks God's laws in a serious way: although he really knows that it is a serious matter, he chooses to do it anyway. In this case, we say that his sin is **mortal**. For a sin to be mortal, it also has to be done after thinking about it. It has to be done on purpose and freely without being forced into it. "Mortal" means something that causes death. Mortal sin kills God's life in the soul. By committing a mortal sin, the person turns away from God and starts heading toward hell.

> "I do not understand my own actions. For I do not do what I want, but I do the very thing I hate. . . . I see in my members another law at war with the law of my mind. . . ."
>
> Romans 7:15, 23

Venial Sin

All of us get lost in small ways. Although we are still headed toward God, we slow down or take a wrong turn. This kind of sin is called **venial sin**. We commit a venial sin when our offense is not serious enough for a mortal sin, but still breaks God's laws. Or perhaps we do not fully realize what we are doing, or we are under pressure. When we commit venial sin, we still love God, but we offend him in little ways.

It is important to try to love God as much as possible by staying away from even venial sins. If we are careless about taking care of the little sicknesses of our souls, we can end up getting really sick by committing mortal sin.

There are four different ways by which we must try to show our love for God: 1) in our thoughts—sometimes our thoughts are not what they should be, for example, when we think something unkind about another; 2) in our words—sometimes our words don't show our love for God (an example of this would be telling a lie); 3) in our actions—our actions can be displeasing to God, for example, in the case of stealing; and finally 4) there are the things that we should have done but did not do, like not doing a chore our parents told us to do. We call these **sins of omission**. To omit something means to leave it undone.

What a happy thing for us that God gives us his grace so that we can win the battle against our wrong desires! We must pray to have good and holy desires. In order for us to receive this grace, Jesus gives us a great sacrament that heals our souls of the damage done to them by our sins. He also gives us special grace not to commit those sins again. That is what we will read about in the next chapter.

Words to Know:

original sin   conscience   sin
actual sin   mortal sin   venial sin
sin of omission

Q. 114 *What is sin?*
Sin is an offense done to God by disobeying his law (CCC 1849–50).

Q. 115 *What was Adam's sin?*
Adam's sin was a grave sin of pride and disobedience. It was the first sin ever committed, so it is called original sin (CCC 397).

Q. 116 *What damage did Adam's sin cause?*
Adam's sin affected him and all men. It removed God's grace and gifts from man, and caused man to suffer illness, death, ignorance, and temptation to sin (CCC 402–405).

Q. 117 *What was original sin for Adam and Eve?*
Original sin for Adam and Eve was a sin they committed when they broke God's command (CCC 404).

Q. 118   *What is original sin?*

Original sin for us is the lack of grace with which we come into existence. It is a result of the sin of our first parents, Adam and Eve. It is not a sin we ourselves commit (CCC 405).

Q. 119   *How is original sin taken away?*

Original sin is taken away by the Sacrament of Baptism (CCC 1263).

Q. 120   *What is actual sin?*

Actual sin is a sin that is committed voluntarily by one who has the use of reason (CCC 1850).

Q. 121   *In how many ways is actual sin committed?*

Actual sin is committed in four ways: in thoughts, in words, in deeds, and in omissions, what we fail to do (CCC 1853).

Q. 122   *How many kinds of actual sin are there?*

Actual sin is of two kinds: mortal and venial (CCC 1854).

Q. 123   *What is mortal sin?*

Mortal sin is an act of disobedience to the law of God in a serious matter, done with full knowledge and deliberate consent (CCC 1855, 1857).

Q. 124   *What is venial sin?*

Venial sin is an act of disobedience to the Law of God in a lesser matter or in a matter in itself serious, but done without full knowledge and consent (CCC 1855, 1862).

CHAPTER 25

Turning Back to God

"Yet even now," says the LORD, "return to me with all your heart, with fasting, with weeping, and with mourning; and rend your hearts and not your garments." Return to the LORD, your God, for he is gracious and merciful, slow to anger, and abounding in steadfast love, and repents of evil.

Joel 2:12–13

Just as God was always ready to forgive the stubborn children of Israel when they turned back to him, he is always waiting for us to turn away from our sins and come back to him to be reconciled with him. There is no sin in the entire world which is too big for Jesus to forgive. Even the biggest mortal sin is not too big for Jesus' love to wash away! But no matter how small our sins are, we still need to keep turning to God to forgive us and to give us his grace so we can grow closer to him.

Jesus gives us a great gift—the Sacrament of **Penance**, which is sometimes called **confession**. It is also sometimes called "**reconciliation**" because it reconciles us with God and with the Church. This sacrament not only forgives our sins but it gives us grace to avoid those sins in the future. It is such a great gift that some people want to become Catholics just so that they can go to confession!

The Prodigal Son

To show the people of Israel and everyone how much Our Heavenly Father is ready to forgive us, Jesus told the following story.

There was a man who had two sons. One day the youngest said to his father, "Father, give me my share of all the money that will come to us after you die."

So the father divided his fortune between them. At once, the younger packed his things and set off on a journey to a faraway land. There he lived a wild life and wasted all his money.

After his money was spent, a famine started in that country and he began to grow very hungry. So he found a job on a farm feeding the pigs. He was willing to eat even the pigs' food, but no one gave him anything.

Suddenly, one day he realized how foolish he was being. "All my father's servants have enough food to eat. I'm no longer worthy to be called his son but at least I can be one of his servants." So he left and went back home.

While he was still a long way from the house, his father saw him and had pity on him. He ran out to meet him, threw his arms around him, and kissed him. Then the son cried, "Father, I have sinned against heaven and against you. I am no longer worthy to be called your son."

118

Right away, his father ordered his servants to bring the best robe and put it on his son and to put a ring on his finger and sandals on his feet. Then he said, "Bring the calf that we have been fattening for a special occasion and kill it. Let us eat and make merry because this son of mine was dead and is alive again. He was lost and is found!"

The Sacrament of Penance

This is the story of your soul. In it, Jesus shows you what happens when you sin, when you come back to God and ask him to forgive you. It is almost as if Jesus sees you coming to confession and runs to meet you there so that he can heal you and give you the grace you need to be good—he wants to help you that much! But in order to be ready to meet Jesus in the Sacrament of Penance, there are certain things that you must do.

Examination of
Your Conscience

First of all, you must examine your conscience. Remember that your conscience judges whether what you have done is good or bad. Now that you know the Ten Commandments, you are able to make your judgments based on them. When you examine, or look at, your conscience, you look back on your thoughts, words, actions, and omissions since your last confession. Have you sometimes not followed the Ten Commandments? If you have trouble remembering what your sins are, ask the Holy Spirit, and he will help you.

Sorrow for Your Sins

Once you know what your sins are, you must be sorry for them. *Feeling* sorry is not neces-

sary or even important because you cannot always feel the way you would like. To *be* sorry for your sins means that you realize that they offend God and deserve punishment. This thought will help you to see how much your sins keep you from really loving God with all your heart.

Intention to
Avoid Your Sins

To be sorry for your sins also means that you do not want to offend God again. So you must make up your mind that you will not commit those sins again. Also you will try to stay away from anything that would lead you to commit those same sins. This is called avoiding the near **occasions of sin**. An *occasion of sin* is a person, place, or thing that would tempt you to sin. For example, if you always misbehave when you sit next to your friend at school, you might decide that you will try to sit somewhere else.

Confession
of Your Sins

After you have examined your conscience and have made up your mind not to commit those sins again, you are ready to meet Jesus in the Sacrament of Penance. You go into the confessional. You may go to confession face to face or behind a screen. After the priest blesses you, he waits for you to tell him your sins. Remember that it is really Jesus whom you are telling. The priest represents Jesus.

"There is joy before the angels of God over one sinner who repents."

Luke 15:10

Your Penance

After the priest has listened to your sins, he might want to give you some advice on how to be better in the future. Then he gives you a penance, which is something you do to make up for the wrong you did. This penance may be a prayer that you are to say or it might be some good action that you must do. Your penance helps you to correct what is wrong in your soul, and, since all sins deserve some kind of punishment, your penance also makes up for some of the punishment your sins deserve.

Absolution

The priest will ask you to say a prayer of contrition or sorrow for your sins. You can find this prayer at the back of this book. Then the priest gives you **absolution**. He and all priests were given this power to forgive sins by Christ himself. It is really Christ who is forgiving you through the priest. He says, "I absolve you from your sins in the name of the Father and of the Son and of the Holy Spirit." At the moment the priest gives you absolution, your sins are forgiven.

After you leave the confessional, as soon as you can you should do the penance the priest has given you. If it is a prayer, you can say it right there in church, maybe even in front of Jesus in the tabernacle. If it is an action, try to do it that day so you will not forget.

Jesus is very pleased to have you come to him in confession. So although it is necessary to receive the Sacrament of Penance only once a year and then only if one is in mortal sin, Jesus does not want you to do only the very least you can do; he wants you to grow closer to him. Because of this, the Church asks you to set aside certain times during the year when you will receive this sacrament. For example, you might want to receive the Sacrament of Penance once a month.

Words to Know:

penance   confession   reconciliation
occasion of sin   absolution

Q. 125   *What is the Sacrament of Penance?*
The Sacrament of Penance was instituted by Jesus Christ to forgive the sins committed after Baptism. This sacrament is also sometimes called confession or reconciliation (CCC 1422, 1428).

Q. 126   *How many things are required to make a good Confession?*
To make a good confession, five things are required: 1) examination of conscience, 2) sorrow for sin, 3) the intention not to commit sin again, 4) the accusation of our sin, 5) satisfaction or penance (CCC 1450).

Q. 127   *How is the examination of conscience done?*

The examination of conscience is done by remembering the sins we have committed in thoughts, words, actions, and omissions against the Commandments of God, beginning from the last good confession (CCC 1454).

Q. 128   *What is sorrow?*

Sorrow or repentance is displeasure and hatred for the sins we have committed, which bring us to form the intention not to sin again (CCC 1451).

Q. 129   *What is absolution?*

Absolution is the judgment by which the priest, in the name of Jesus Christ, forgives the penitent his sins, saying, "I absolve you from your sins in the Name of the Father and of the Son and of the Holy Spirit. *Amen*" (CCC 1449).

Q. 130   *What is the penance given in the Sacrament of Penance?*

The penance is a good work imposed by the confessor for the punishment and correction of the sinner and to take away some of the temporal punishment due to sin (CCC 1459).

Q. 131   *What is an occasion of sin?*

An occasion of sin is a person, place, or thing that puts us in danger of sinning (1 Jn 2:15–17).

Q. 132   *Are we obliged to avoid occasions of sin?*

Yes, we are obliged to avoid occasions of sin because we are obliged to avoid sin itself (1 Tim 5:14).

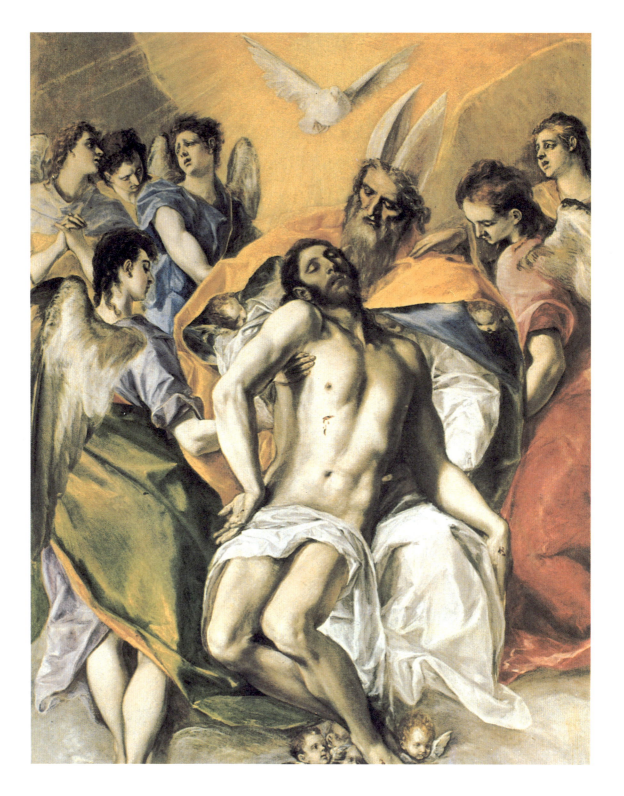

122

CHAPTER 26

The Holy Spirit

Do you not know that you are God's temple and that God's Spirit dwells in you?

1 Corinthians 3:16

The God of Abraham

If you had asked Abraham what he knew of God, he would have told you that God is infinite, all powerful, all good, knows all things, and that he can be believed and trusted. Also, he would have told you that God is one. In fact, one of the things that made Abraham and his descendants different from their neighbors was that they worshipped only one God while their neighbors worshipped many gods.

Then suppose you had asked Abraham about the three Persons in the one God that he worshipped. He would not have known about that. It was not until Jesus came and revealed it that we learned about the three Persons in God.

Sometimes people get a little confused and they think that Christians worship three Gods: the Father, the Son, and the Holy Spirit. In fact, however, we worship the very same God that Abraham and the Jews worshipped. We just know more about him now.

The Holy Trinity

We call the three Persons in one God the Blessed Trinity or the **Holy Trinity**. How there can be three Persons in one God is a mystery.

Remember a mystery is something that God has told us, which our human minds can never completely understand.

Although we can never completely understand the Trinity, we can learn more about it. The First Person of the Holy Trinity is God the Father, the Creator of heaven and earth. His "Word" is his Son. We say of the Son that he is "Light from Light, true God from true God, eternally begotten of the Father." That means that he is in every way equal to the Father. He is the Second Person of the Holy Trinity, God the Son, who became man in the Divine Person of Jesus.

God the Father and God the Son have loved each other from all eternity. This love that they have is so perfect and so complete that it is another Person, equal to the Father and the Son. This is God the **Holy Spirit**, the Third Person of the Holy Trinity.

The Holy Spirit

Because the Holy Spirit is the *love* between God the Father and God the Son, whenever God gives us something out of *love*, we say that it is the work of the Holy Spirit. And since everything God gives us is given in love, the Holy Spirit is always active in our world.

The first time the Holy Spirit came into your soul was at your Baptism. Then your body became his temple because he began to live in you. He made it possible for you to love God and others. He will come in a new way when you are confirmed. When you receive the Sacrament of Confirmation, the Holy Spirit will make you an even stronger follower of Jesus. Until your Confirmation, you can ask the Holy Spirit to fill your heart with love and help you to grow closer to Jesus, and he will do this.

The Holy Spirit from The Beginning of Time

The Holy Spirit has been active from the very beginning of time. It was he who was speaking through the writers of the Old Testament (which is the first part of the Bible from Adam and Eve to the birth of Jesus Christ). It was he who was speaking to the children of Israel through the prophets. For example, when Isaiah said that the Messiah would be a descendant of David, it was the Holy Spirit who gave them that knowledge.

When the time came for the Son of God to come into the world, it was through the Holy Spirit's power that Mary was made Christ's mother. And when Jesus was baptized by his cousin, John, it was the Holy Spirit who came down in the form of a dove.

Then, after Jesus ascended into heaven his friends were left to carry on his work. When they wanted to write down the things he had said and done, it was the Holy Spirit who guided them.

The Holy Spirit and The Birth of the Church

Before Jesus ascended into heaven, he was with his apostles in Jerusalem. "Stay in the city, until you are clothed with power from above," he told them. He also promised that after his departure from this world he would not leave them orphans, but he would send them the Holy Spirit (also called the Paraclete, the Counsellor, or the Spirit of Truth) who would guide them into all truth. And this Holy Spirit would fill their hearts with great joy.

After this, he led them a short distance outside the city and, after blessing them, rose up into the heavens. Joyfully, his friends returned to Jerusalem and gathered together with his mother, Mary, to wait and pray for the power that Jesus had promised.

After nine days of praying, suddenly a mighty wind filled the house where they were staying. Then there appeared tongues of fire over each person in the house. Everyone was filled with the power from above—the Holy Spirit filled them with his strength. It was the feast of Pentecost. This was the birthday of the Church, which you will read about in the next chapter. You will also see how the Holy Spirit, as well as guiding you, is at work guiding the Church.

Words to Know:

Holy Trinity   Holy Spirit

Come, Holy Spirit, fill the hearts of your faithful. Enkindle in them the fire of your love.

Pentecost, Alleluia verse

Q. 133   *Is there only one God?*

Yes, there is only one God, who exists as three equal and distinct Persons. We call these persons the Holy Trinity (CCC 233, 253).

Q. 134   *What are the three Persons of the Holy Trinity called?*

The three Persons of the Holy Trinity are called the Father, the Son, and the Holy Spirit (CCC 233, 254).

Q. 135   *Is each Person of the Holy Trinity God?*

Yes, each Person of the Holy Trinity is God (CCC 253).

Q. 136   *Who is the First Person of the Holy Trinity?*

The First Person of the Holy Trinity is God the Father (CCC 238–40, 255).

Q. 137   *Who is the Second Person of the Holy Trinity?*

The Second Person of the Holy Trinity is God the Son (CCC 240–42, 255).

Q. 138   *Who is the Third Person of the Holy Trinity?*

The Third Person of the Holy Trinity is God the Holy Spirit (CCC 243–44, 255).

Q. 139   *Are the three Divine Persons equal, or is one greater than the others?*

The three Divine Persons, since they are only one God, are equal in every respect and possess equally and in common every perfection and every action (CCC 253, 255, 266–67).

CHAPTER 27

The Church of Christ

"And I tell you, you are Peter, and on this rock I will build my church, and the powers of death shall not prevail against it."

Matthew 16:18

The People of God

When God made his covenant with the people of Israel, he said, "I will take you for *my people* and I will be your God." He was not just going to make Moses and Aaron holy; he wanted to make the whole people of Israel holy.

But that covenant was a preparation for the **new covenant** of Jesus, which is perfect. Jesus has made one people out of Jews and gentiles from all over the world (including you) and he wants to make us holy as a community. We are the people of the "**new Israel**" or the new **People of God**. Another name for the new People of God is the Church.

To be part of a holy people means that we are not just each one a pilgrim on his own. We are travelling to heaven together and we need to help each other get there. Each of us can help.

Because the Church is holy and through her sacraments she can make us holy, we her members, (although we are still sinners and in constant need of purification), become holy. We, the People of God, are pilgrims who have not yet reached our goal, but we are on our way *toward* God.

The Mystical Body of Christ

But the Church is more than a group of people. Because the Holy Spirit is in each of us through Baptism, he draws us together so closely that we become like a real body that is alive.

Before his Ascension Christ said, "I am with you always even to the end of the world." He is with us in his Church, especially through the Eucharist, his Body. By partaking of the Eucharist we become so closely united to Christ that we even become part of his Body. St. Paul says that the Church is Christ's Body and Christ is her head. She is called the "**Mystical Body of Christ**." "Mystical" means that it is a spiritual, not a physical, body. It is the Holy Spirit who gives life to the body.

Everyone who is baptized and has the life of grace in his soul is a member of the Mystical Body of Christ. The body has many parts, like arms and legs. Do you know what it means for you to be part of this body? It means that you are connected in a *spiritual* and *very real* way with Jesus and every other single person in the

> *"And men will come from east and west, and from north and south, and sit at table in the kingdom of God."*
>
> *Luke 13:29*

Church (including the persons in heaven and purgatory). This means that your prayers and sacrifices can help those who need them and that theirs can help you.

Being a member of the Mystical Body of Christ also means that if you are holy, it is good for the whole body, just as if your arm is healthy it helps your whole body to work well. In the same way, when one of the members of the Mystical Body of Christ is sick from sin, the whole body suffers, just as your body would suffer from a broken arm.

And finally, being part of the Mystical Body of Christ means that not everyone has the same part to play in the body but each part is important so that the whole body will work well. You might be an eye, or an arm, or even a little finger, but whatever part you have to play, Jesus has given you the talents and gifts that are needed for that part.

A Priestly People

Do you remember why Jesus was the greatest priest? It is because he was the perfect offerer of the greatest and most perfect Sacrifice of himself. Because you are a part of Christ's Mystical Body through your Baptism, you can share in his role as priest!

All priests offer something up to God. Jesus calls some men to be his *special* priests. He gives these priests the power to change bread and wine into his Body and Blood and offer it up to the Father. No one else is given this power.

But Jesus calls you to share in his priesthood in a different way which is still very important.

What can you offer up to God? At Mass, with the priest, you can offer up Jesus and yourself to the Father. And every day, you can offer yourself to God by praying and by living a holy life.

A Kingly People

Do you remember that Jesus was called the "King of the Jews"—and the Kingdom which Jesus came to bring is for everyone and is a spiritual Kingdom? Jesus is truly a king because, as a result of his death and Resurrection, God the Father has placed every single thing under Jesus' power—all creation. Jesus is really ruling the whole universe—nothing happens without his knowledge and permission!

Since you are a part of Christ's Body through your Baptism, you become sons and daughters of a King—a royal people! You spread your Father's Kingdom by making your conscience rule over your actions to make them good and unselfish. In this way, you can serve Jesus in other people. To serve Jesus in other people is to realize that whenever you do something for someone else, you are really doing it for Jesus. The other people will follow your example and will come to serve Jesus as their King too. Jesus wants you to spread his Kingdom by your holy life.

A Prophetic People

Do you remember why Jesus is the greatest prophet? This is because he could bring God's word to us in the best way possible since he *is* God.

The parts of Christ's Mystical Body share his

role as prophet. You do this by using the talents that Jesus has given you to spread his word that you learn at home, in school, and in church to your family and friends. You can also spread his word by the joyful way that you live your life. Jesus wants everyone to belong to the People of God and he wants you to help!

The Church's Shepherds

Jesus called us his sheep. Do you know what sheep are like? By themselves, they can easily get hurt or lost. Because of this, they need a shepherd to lead them. A shepherd loves his sheep and cares for them. Jesus is our shepherd.

We are Jesus' sheep; we need to be led and helped to find him. To make sure that we would find him after his Ascension, Jesus made the apostles the shepherds of his people until he comes again. The apostles passed this power on to others, called "**bishops**." Our bishop looks after us, his flock of sheep.

But even the shepherds themselves needed a leader. So Jesus made one of his shepherds a leader of the rest. His name was Peter. Peter became bishop of Rome, and each successor of his is called the **Pope**.

Guardians of the Truth

After Christ's twelve apostles died, the duty of all the bishops after them was to teach all that Christ had revealed and all that the apostles (the true witnesses of Christ) had taught. They were to guard Christ's teaching and pass it down to others without taking away or adding anything. But Jesus knew that our shepherds were only human and could make mistakes about his message. Can you imagine what would happen to Christ's message if it had to be passed down from person to person for nearly two thousand years without any special help to guard it? We would almost certainly receive a

very different teaching than the one Jesus wants us to have!

So in order to make sure that the good news heard by us would really be his own, Jesus sent the Holy Spirit to guide the shepherds of the Church so that they could teach the truth. The Pope is the chief shepherd of the Church. The Holy Spirit protects him from error when he teaches all the People of God something important for them to believe (we call these teachings of faith) or what is sinful or good (we call these teachings on morals). The teachings of all of the other bishops, when they instruct the People of God together with the Pope, are also protected by the Holy Spirit.

We call this protection **infallibility**. Infallibility is a guarantee to us that when the Pope alone or the Pope with the bishops teach us in matters of faith and morals, we can know for certain this teaching is free from error. We can be sure it is really Christ's teaching. But even when the words of the Pope and the bishops are not guarded by infallibility, we must still listen to them and obey them.

Other Christians

From the time that Jesus started his Church nearly two thousand years ago, many things have happened to her. One of the saddest things happened when large groups of people in many countries left the Catholic Church because they thought that she was no longer Jesus' Church. Sometimes this happened because of the sinful actions of many Catholics. These people who left started their own churches. That is why there are different churches today, that of the Lutherans, Methodists, Presbyterians, Baptists, and Anglicans. This is sad because Jesus wanted all of his followers to be united in his one Catholic Church.

All that happened long ago. Most people who are members of these churches today do not really know about the Catholic Church and that she has *all* the sacraments and the *whole* teaching of Jesus. They are trying to love and serve God in the way they know best. Jesus is guiding his followers who are outside the Catholic Church, and because they are bap-

tized, they are part of his family, too. You should respect them and love them as your brothers and sisters because they are the brothers and sisters of Jesus. But you should also pray that all may be together again as Jesus wants in his one Catholic Church.

Words to Know:

New Covenant   New Israel
People of God
Mystical Body of Christ
bishop   Pope   infallibility

Let us pray for all our brothers and sisters who share our faith in Jesus Christ, that God may gather and keep together in one Church all those who seek the truth with sincerity.

General Intercessions for Holy Week

Q. 140 *What is the Church?*

The Church is the community of disciples, the People of God, who profess the same faith and the teaching of Jesus Christ, share in his sacraments, and obey the pastors whom he has appointed (CCC 751).

Q. 141 *Who founded the Church?*

Jesus Christ founded the Church (CCC 763).

Q. 142 *Who are the chief pastors of the Church?*

The chief pastors of the Church are the Pope, who is the Vicar of Christ, and the bishops united with him (CCC 880).

Q. 143 *Who is the Pope?*

The Pope is the successor of Saint Peter, the bishop of Rome, the visible head of the entire Church on earth, with Christ as the invisible head of the Church (CCC 881–82).

Q. 144 *What do the Pope and the bishops united with him make up?*

The Pope and the bishops united with him make up the chief teachers in the Church. They have received from Jesus Christ the mission of teaching the truths and Laws of God to all men (CCC 888).

Q. 145 *Can the Pope and the bishops united with him err in defining teaching on faith and morals?*

No, the Pope and the bishops united with him cannot err in defining teaching on faith and morals: they are infallible, which is a protection against error, assured by Christ and given through the Holy Spirit (CCC 890).

Q. 146 *Can the Pope, by himself, err in defining teaching on faith and morals?*

No, the Pope, by himself, cannot err in defining teaching on faith and morals (CCC 891).

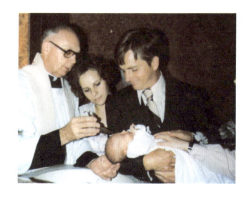

CHAPTER 28

Channels of Grace

And from his fulness have we all received, grace upon grace.

John 1:16

Grace

You have read that Adam and Eve lost **grace** for themselves and for all of us and that Jesus won it back, but do you know what grace is? Here are some of the things you should know about it: 1) Grace is not something you can see or touch but it is still very real. 2) Grace is *not* something that God owes to us. 3) He gives it to us as a free gift because he loves us. 4) Grace does its work in our souls if we say "yes" to it. 5) Also, grace heals our souls from the damage that original sin and our own personal sins have done to them. 6) Grace gives us the power to break bad habits and to say "no" to temptations. 7) Without grace, we would be unable to love God or neighbor, or even to do one good thing. 8) We can and should increase the grace in our souls. 9) Finally, and most importantly, as a share in God's own life, grace raises us up to be able to live a life higher than the one here on earth, that is, our life in heaven.

Artists have often painted grace to look like the rays of the sun. That image helps us to understand what grace is like. Rays come from the sun; in fact they are part of the sun. In the same way grace comes from God; it is divine. Like grace, the sun's rays are not something you can touch. They flow from the sun to make new life grow from the earth. In the same way,

grace flows from the life, death, and Resurrection of Jesus and gives us new life.

The Sacraments

Imagine that grace is made up of many rays, streaming throughout the world from the life, death, and Resurrection of Jesus. Jesus, who is guiding and directing the rays, lets them fall everywhere but most of them he channels through the **sacraments**. The sacraments are the way Jesus has chosen to give us the grace that he has gained for us.

A sacrament is a sign. A sign is something that can be seen or heard which gives a message about something else. For example, when you see a red light, the message is "Stop." And when you hear the telephone ring, the message is "someone wants to talk to me." The sacraments are signs too. Each sacrament gives us the message that Jesus is giving us his grace in some way. For example, in the Sacrament of Baptism, when you see water being poured on a baby's head and hear the words the priest is saying, the message is, "sin is being washed away."

But the sacraments are *more* than signs. Jesus works through them to make the message

> I saw water flowing from the right side of the Temple, Alleluia.
>
> It brought God's life and his salvation, and the people sang in joyful praise: Alleluia, Alleluia.
>
> Antiphon from the Easter Vigil Mass

really happen! They *really* give us the grace of which they are signs. For example, Baptism *really* washes away original sin from the baby's soul.

The people of Israel had signs too, such as laying their hands on an animal's head before it was sacrificed. The message here was that the person's sins were being transferred to the animal. But it was just a sign. It did not really remove his sins because it was not until Jesus' life, death, and Resurrection that certain signs could forgive sins and give grace. *Now*, our sacrament or sign for the forgiveness of sins really does forgive them!

There are seven sacraments. You have probably received three of them already: Baptism, Penance, and Holy Eucharist. Now we will talk about all seven of them.

Baptism

The day of your **Baptism** was your birthday as a child of God. It started you on your pilgrimage to heaven. Through this sacrament, God freed your soul from the effects of original sin, any other sin, and gave you the grace to live a holy life. You became a member of Christ's Church. Because of your Baptism, you have a right and the duty for the rest of your life to receive certain other sacraments, especially the Eucharist.

Also, at Baptism you first became a temple of the Holy Spirit. God came to be in you in a different way than he does in unbaptized persons!

The Holy Eucharist

The Holy Eucharist is the central sacrament of Catholic life because it is Jesus himself. Jesus in the Eucharist is the Food we need to continue our journey on earth on our way to heaven. When we receive Jesus properly, he gives us the grace to love God with all our hearts and to love others as we love ourselves. That is the way to heaven.

Penance

Just as our bodies get sick and need to be healed, our souls suffer sickness as a result of our sins. Through this wonderful sacrament, Jesus heals our souls of sins committed after Baptism. He also gives us the grace necessary to avoid those sins in the future.

In the last chapter you saw that we are part of the Mystical Body of Christ and also that our sins hurt this Body. Well, through the Sacrament of Penance, we are healed of our sins, and the hurt we have done to the Body is healed.

Confirmation

Soon you will receive another sacrament: the Sacrament of **Confirmation**. Another name for Confirmation could be "making stronger." Through Confirmation, Jesus sends the Holy Spirit, who gives you the grace to be an even stronger follower of Jesus by your words and actions. Confirmation permanently marks you as Jesus' strong witness, which means that, by your words and your example, you are actually helping to spread the Kingdom of God, starting with your friends and family.

Holy Orders

If you are a boy, Jesus might be calling you to come very close to him in a special way by becoming a priest when you grow up. Then you would receive a sacrament called **Holy Orders**. Through Holy Orders, Jesus would make you his permanent deputy or minister. After you received this sacrament, Jesus would work through you in a special way to make other people holy.

The priest is able to bring Christ's grace to people in a powerful way through the Mass. At Mass, Jesus changes the bread and wine into his Body and Blood through the priest's words and actions. Then the priest can feed the people with Living Bread for their journey to heaven. Also, in the name of Jesus and acting in his person, the priest has the power to forgive people's sins so that they will be healed in order to continue their journey. What a wonderful thing it is for the Church to have men who will give their lives to Jesus as priests! If we had no priests, we would not be able to receive forgiveness of our sins through the Sacrament of Penance and we would not be able to receive Jesus in Holy Communion. The priesthood is so important that in countries where the Church is persecuted some men have even risked their lives to become priests and celebrate Mass!

Marriage

There is a good chance that you will get married when you grow up. As soon as two people get married, they become pilgrims together in a special way. They make a little covenant of their own. Their life's work is to help each

other and their children follow Christ on earth and get to heaven. They must try their best to love each other faithfully, even in hard times, to give their children much love, and to be a cheerful, happy, and good family. But they must be careful not to spoil their children because the children would become selfish and unhappy people and have a harder time getting to heaven. All this is very hard work for a man and woman. Jesus knows how hard it is. So he gives married people a sacrament of their own—the Sacrament of **Marriage**. Through this sacrament, Jesus helps married people be good husbands and wives, mothers and fathers.

Anointing of the Sick

Have you ever been very sick or have you ever seen sick people in a hospital? There are boys and girls your age who must go to the hospital. Being sick can be hard because pain often makes people tired and afraid. Jesus often cured the sick and showed his love for them. He gives a sacrament to people who are very sick or old, especially to those in danger of death. It is called the Sacrament of the **Anointing of the Sick**. The priest anoints the person's head with oil and says some prayers. This sacrament gives the sick person the grace to accept his sickness as coming from God and helps him to get ready to meet Jesus when he dies. It will also forgive his venial sins and mortal sins if he is truly sorry for them but is unable to confess them. It can help him in his suffering and can even heal his body if that is God's will.

Words to Know:

grace   sacrament
Baptism   Confirmation
Holy Orders   Marriage
Anointing of the Sick

Q. 147   *What are the sacraments?*

The sacraments are signs of grace instituted by Jesus Christ to make us holy (CCC 1114, 1123, 1128).

Q. 148   *Why are the sacraments signs of grace?*

The sacraments are signs of grace because those aspects of them that we can perceive with our senses signify or indicate the invisible grace that they give (CCC 1123, 1127).

Q. 149   *Who gave the sacraments the power of giving grace?*

Jesus Christ, true God and true man, gave the sacraments the power of giving grace, which he himself merited for us by his Passion and death (CCC 1116, 1127).

Q. 150   *What should we do to receive and preserve the grace of the sacraments?*

To receive the grace of the sacraments, we must be ready for them and open to them. To preserve the grace of the sacraments, we must cooperate by doing good and avoiding evil (CCC 1123, 1128).

Q. 151   *What is Baptism?*

Baptism is the sacrament by which people are made children of God and members of Jesus' Church through the power of the Holy Spirit, who washes away original sin and any actual sin, and gives the life of grace (CCC 1213, 1262).

Q. 152   *What is Confirmation?*

Confirmation is the sacrament that makes us more perfect Christians and witnesses of Christ by the gifts of the Holy Spirit (CCC 1285).

Q. 153   *What is the Sacrament of Matrimony?*

The Sacrament of Matrimony is Christian marriage. This sacrament unites a man and a woman permanently. It also gives them special graces in order to live in a holy way and to raise and educate their children in a Christian manner (CCC 1601).

Q. 154   *What duties do husbands and wives assume?*

Husbands and wives assume the duties of helping each other with un-failing affection in their temporal and spiritual necessities, and of raising and forming their children well, especially in the faith (CCC 1641).

Q. 155   *What is Holy Orders?*

Holy Orders is the sacrament which gives a man the power to carry out the sacred actions regarding the salvation of souls (CCC 1536).

Q. 156   *What is the Anointing of the Sick?*

The Anointing of the Sick is the sacrament instituted for the spiritual and also the bodily strengthening of Christians who are gravely ill. The Anointing of the Sick increases sanctifying grace. It takes away venial sins and also the mortal sins, if the sick person is unable to confess them. It gives the Christian the strength to bear patiently the evil he suffers, to resist all temptations, and, if such is the case, to die a holy death; and finally, it also helps to regain bodily health, if this is good for the soul (CCC 1499, 1508, 1520, 1523).

CHAPTER 29

Our Mother, Mary

And a great portent appeared in heaven, a woman clothed with the sun, with the moon under her feet, and on her head a crown of twelve stars.

Revelation 12:1

The Second Eve

Have you ever heard about the **"second" Adam and Eve**? Jesus is called the "second" Adam. The first Adam disobeyed God by eating the forbidden fruit, but Jesus obeyed his Father by dying on the Cross for us. Adam brought sin into the world, but Jesus, the second Adam, conquered sin. Adam lost grace for us, but Jesus won it back again.

Now who do you suppose the "second" Eve is? She is Mary, Christ's mother. Eve disobeyed God, but Mary obeyed God when he asked her to be the mother of his Son. Eve helped Adam to sin by bringing him the fruit from the forbidden tree, but Mary helps Jesus in his saving mission. He has honored Mary by allowing her to help him.

Jesus let Mary help him by being his mother: by carrying him in her womb and then by caring for him when he was a child growing up. Later Mary helped Jesus when he was dying on the Cross. She stood close by and, although she suffered greatly to see her son beaten and killed, she offered him to the Father for our sins.

Immaculate Mary

Because Mary was asked by God to play such an important part in his work of saving us, God gave her a very special gift. Since a mother who had even the smallest sin would not have been the right mother or teacher for the Son of God, God kept Mary free from original sin from the first moment of her life. We call her *Immaculate* because that means that her soul is spotless. Mary never committed a single sin— throughout her whole life she always said "yes"

So, love Our Lady, dear young people and children! Pray to her every day! May the Blessed Virgin, prayed to, loved, and imitated, help you to remain good and happy in a holy way!

Pope John Paul II, General Audience, May 9, 1979

to God and did his will. Because Mary was conceived with no trace of sin, she is called the Immaculate Conception.

The Assumption

Since Mary was so close to Jesus and since she was his own much loved mother, Jesus wanted her to share in the honors and glories of his Resurrection as soon as possible. So when her time on this earth came to an end, Jesus took her—both body and soul—to heaven to be with him forever. We call this the **Assumption** or the "taking up" of Mary into heaven.

Mary's Assumption is also a reminder to us. If, like Mary, we try to offer up our lives and our sufferings, we will also share in Christ's glory with our bodies and souls in heaven!

Our Heavenly Mother

Just as Christ's work to save us is still going on, so he is still allowing his mother to share that work. From the Cross he gave her to us as our mother when he said, "This is your mother," to his disciple John. Therefore she is called "Mother of the Church." She is watching over all of us pilgrims with a mother's care and love. When we pray to her, she asks Jesus, who is always ready to grant her wishes, to help us. Mary will continue to help us until the end of the world and she will lead us all safely home to heaven.

Mary Leads to Jesus

If we pray to and love Mary, she will always lead us to Jesus. Once there was a wedding feast at Cana. Jesus and his mother were invited. When they ran out of wine, Mary noticed it. She told Jesus about it and then sent the waiters to him telling them, "Do whatever he tells you." Jesus told them to fill the wine jars with water. When the head waiter and bridegroom tasted it, they realized it had been turned into wine! In the same way, when we go to Mary she asks Jesus to help us and then says to us, "Do whatever my son tells you." Then, if we listen to Jesus and obey him, we will be helped.

Words to Know:

second Adam   second Eve   Assumption

Q. 157   *Was anyone among the descendants of Adam ever preserved from original sin?*

Besides Jesus, Mary his Mother has been preserved from original sin. Because she was chosen to be the Mother of God, she was "full of grace" (Lk 1:28), free from the stain of original sin from the first instant of her existence. The Church celebrates Mary as the Immaculate Conception (CCC 490–91).

CHAPTER 30

We Reach Our Goal

And I saw the holy city, new Jerusalem, coming down out of heaven from God, prepared as a bride adorned for her husband.

Revelation 21:2

The Particular Judgment

One day you will reach the end of your pilgrimage and God your Father will call you home to be with him. When you die, you will meet Jesus, who will judge your life. We call this the **Particular Judgment** because it concerns only you and Jesus. Jesus will look at all of your thoughts, words, actions, and omissions from the time when you were old enough to choose good over evil.

And since only those without any sin can enter heaven, some of us will need to be purified by suffering for a time in **purgatory**. Through purgatory, Jesus will heal our souls and help us to make up for the many sins that we have committed on earth.

Some very sad people will not want to meet Jesus when they die. These are people who have shut him out of their lives by mortal sin for which they are not sorry. Since they have rejected Jesus Christ of their own free will and cut themselves off from his love forever, they have chosen to be forever with the bad angels in hell.

Hope and Joy

Do we fear the Last Judgment? The idea of having even our thoughts judged by Jesus can make us afraid. This is because we are all sinners and we are ashamed of our sins. We are also afraid of being punished for them.

It is true that we deserve punishment, but we may also hope in the mercy of Jesus. He wants to save us. And with a look of infinite love he will see all our efforts at obeying him, loving him and others, receiving the sacraments, and praying. He will see how we have used the grace he has given us. The more we grow in love of him on earth the greater will be our joy when we see him in heaven.

The General Judgment

Finally on a day and in a way that no one knows, the world will end, and Jesus will come to gather before him all the people on earth and all those in heaven, purgatory, and hell. Jesus will judge every person who has ever been born. Each will go either to heaven or to hell for

eternity. Only those people will go to hell who have chosen to shut God out of their lives by mortal sin. We call this the **General Judgment** because every soul will be judged.

The Resurrection of the Body

Has anyone ever told you that you will become an angel when you die? That is not true. Angels are complete without their bodies but human beings are not. Our souls were not made to exist by themselves. Your soul is only part of you and your body is such a good and beautiful thing that God would not throw it away.

At the end of the world Jesus will raise up the bodies of everyone who has ever existed and unite them to their souls again. We call this the resurrection of the body. But although your resurrected body will be the same body you have now, it will be different somehow. It will be glorified and beautiful and will live forever.

Unending Joy

Perhaps you have thought of heaven as either boring or a place of separation. Nothing could be further from the truth. You will be reunited with all those you love and they will love you more than before. Think of it this way: the most beautiful place in the whole world or the happiest moment of your life cannot even come close to the beauty and happiness of heaven. Above all you will be united with Jesus Christ in glory, and you will see God!

St. Paul tells us: "Eye has not seen, ear has not heard nor has it entered into the heart of

> Beloved boys and girls, I conclude by saying to you, keep yourselves worthy of Jesus whom you receive! Be innocent and generous! Try to make life beautiful for everyone with obedience, kindness, good manners! The secret of joy is goodness!
>
> Pope John Paul II, Address given in St. Peter's Basilica on the feast of Corpus Christi, June 14, 1979

man, what God has prepared for those who love him" (1 Corinthians 2:9).

Meanwhile, before that wonderful time comes, we are still on the way. And, although nothing will be perfect until we get to heaven, the holier we become, the more we will have a foretaste of heaven on earth.

Just as Jesus has invited Mary, so he also invites us to help him bring our brothers and sisters to heaven. If they see in your life goodness and kindness, sharing, patience, and cheerfulness, they will be drawn to Christ. He will work through you so that others will also want to become pilgrims to heaven. And then Christ in his great mercy will reunite you with them and fill your hearts with unending joy.

Words to Know:

Particular Judgment
purgatory   General Judgment
resurrection of the body

Q. 158   *Will Jesus Christ ever return visibly to this earth?*
Yes, Jesus Christ will return visibly to this earth to judge the living and the dead at the end of the world (CCC 671).

Q. 159 *Will Jesus Christ wait until the end of the world to judge us?*

Jesus Christ will not wait until the end of the world to judge us, but he will judge each one of us immediately after death at the Particular Judgment (CCC 1021–22).

Q. 160 *On what will Jesus Christ judge us?*

Jesus Christ will judge us on the good and evil that we have done in life, including our thoughts and the things we failed to do (CCC 1022).

Q. 161 *After the Particular Judgment, what happens to the soul?*

After the Particular Judgment, if a person is without sin and without a debt of punishment for sin, his soul goes into heaven. If a person has some venial sin or temporal punishment due for sin, his soul goes into purgatory to be purified. If a person is in mortal sin, as a changeless rebel against God, his soul goes into hell (CCC 1022).

Q. 162 *What is Purgatory?*

Purgatory is the temporary suffering of the lack of the vision of God and also of other punishments that remove from the soul the remains of venial sin. Purgatory holds the punishments that were not endured for sin in earthly life, and makes the soul worthy to see God (CCC 1030–32).

Q. 163 *What does "resurrection of the body" mean?*

The "resurrection of the body" means that at the Last Judgment our body will be reunited to our soul, by the power of God, in order for us to participate during eternal life in the reward or punishment that our souls have merited (CCC 988, 997–98).

Q. 164 *Who may go to heaven?*

Every good person, who loves God, serves him faithfully, and dies in his grace, may go to heaven, either directly if he is without a debt of sin, or after a purification in purgatory (CCC 1023).

Q. 165 *Why should we want to go to heaven?*

We should want to go to heaven because in heaven we will perfectly possess God, who alone can make us eternally and perfectly happy (CCC 1023–24).

Advent and Christmas Supplement

> Watch therefore, for you do not know on what day your Lord is coming.
>
> Matthew 24:42

Even many people who do not believe in Jesus celebrate his birthday by buying Christmas trees and exchanging presents. And we, who do believe in Jesus, often look forward to Christmas for months. We are filled with the excitement of presents, carols, parties, and cookies. But sometimes we can become so busy with these things that we forget what an incredible and wonderful thing happened—God became a man and nothing has been the same since or will ever be the same again!

Advent

Because Jesus' birth means so much for us, we count the days before it. It is a time of waiting and wishing that he were with us even more. The Church calls this time **Advent**, which means "coming." During Advent we, like the people of Israel, can long for the coming of the one who will change the world, the Redeemer. We can also look forward to Jesus' coming at the end of the world.

Jesus is really with us so we should be joyful during Advent but we should also spend these four weeks preparing our hearts to make sure that Jesus has a home there. It is good to prepare our hearts in a special way for his birthday. Spending some extra time with Jesus in prayer,

receiving the Sacrament of Penance, and going to Mass on a weekday are all ways of doing this.

We should also think of how we can help Jesus be born in the hearts of our families and friends. We can do this by trying to be helpful to them.

Here is what was happening before the first Christmas:

One day, a Jewish man and his wife were walking along the dusty road to Bethlehem. They had received an order from Caesar Augustus (who, as you will remember, was the Roman ruler of the Jews) to go to the city of their ancestors to be counted. This way, Caesar would know how many people of Israel were in his kingdom. Since the man and woman were descendants of David, they were going to the city of David's birth, Bethlehem.

If you had seen them walking along on the road to Bethlehem, you might have noticed some things about them; they were very special! For one thing, they were very good, and that must have shown in their peaceful faces and in the kind and considerate way in which they treated each other. In fact, God had kept the woman's soul free from sin from the first moment of her life in the womb of her mother. The effects of original sin had never even touched her soul. You also might have noticed

that the woman was going to have a baby. This baby was very special. He was the one the Jews had been waiting for. By now, you have guessed the names of this woman and man: Mary and Joseph.

Christmas

Finally, they arrived in Bethlehem. The city was crowded with other descendants of David who came to enroll their families. Because of this, all the inns were filled. They had no choice but to spend the night in a stable. Mary gave birth to her baby there. She wrapped him up tightly in the strips of cloth that the Jews used to wrap newborn babies. And then she placed him in a manger. (A manger is a trough from which animals eat.)

Soon, from the fields near Bethlehem, arrived a group of Jewish shepherds, such as King David had been. "We've come to see the child," one probably said.

Then the shepherds told their story. It must have gone something like this: "We were watching our sheep tonight when we saw a glorious light shine and an angel appear. We were very much afraid but then the angel said, 'Be not afraid for I bring you good news of great joy! To you is born this day in the City of David a Savior, who is Christ the Lord. And here is a sign for you: you will find a baby wrapped in swaddling clothes and lying in a manger.'

"And then the whole sky was filled with angels," the shepherds continued excitedly. "They were all praising God and saying, 'Glory to God in the highest and on earth peace among men with whom he is pleased!' So we hurried to see him and here he is!"

Mary and Joseph were full of wonder at the story of the shepherds. And the shepherds went back to their fields praising and glorifying God for these wonderful events.

Soon after Jesus was born, his parents took him to the temple in Jerusalem to offer him to God, his Father, and also to offer a sacrifice of two young pigeons. This was the Jewish custom.

There was a very holy man named Simeon living in Jerusalem. It was revealed to him by the Holy Spirit that he would not die until he saw the Christ, the one promised to the people of Israel. Simeon was in the temple when Mary, Joseph, and Jesus came in. He took the child up in his arms and inspired by the Holy Spirit he said, "Now, Lord, you can let me die in peace, because I have seen the salvation which you have prepared; a light for the gentiles and the glory of your people, Israel!"

Once again, Mary and Joseph marveled at these words of a man who had never seen Jesus before that moment! Simeon blessed them and then spoke his last words to Mary. "This child is destined for the fall and the rising of many in Israel. The secret thoughts of many will be known. And a sword will pierce your own soul."

And as Simeon had said, this child was not only for the Jews. There were some others to arrive: the gentiles. One day three gentiles from the East came to Jerusalem. These men were wise and had been studying the prophecies about the Messiah. They went to King Herod and asked, "Where is he who has been born king of the Jews? We have seen his star in the east and have come to worship him."

Like Saul, Herod was worried that a new king would take his place. But he did not say anything to the wise men about this. He went to the Jewish priests, who had studied the prophecies. "Where is this king supposed to be born?" he asked.

"In Bethlehem of Judea," they answered.

So Herod sent the wise men to Bethlehem.

"Search hard for the child," he said, "and when you have found him, let me know, so that I, too, can go and worship him."

The wise men followed the star to Bethlehem. They were filled with great joy when they saw it stop above where the child was. They entered the house and saw Jesus with his mother, Mary. At once, they fell to their knees and worshipped the new King. And then they offered him gifts of gold, frankincense, and myrrh.

Then the wise men were warned in a dream not to return to Herod. So they departed for their own country using a different route.

Just as Jesus was born for the wise men and other gentiles of that time, he was also born for you. He is the Messiah, the Savior that all generations waited for. That is why you celebrate his birthday every year. Christmas should be a time for you to grow closer to Jesus.

Words to Know:

Advent

Behold a rose of Judah
From tender branch has sprung
From Jesse's lineage coming
As men of old have sung
It came a flower bright
Amid the cold of winter
When half-spent was the night.

Christmas Hymn

148

Lent and Easter Supplement

Then Jesus was led up by the Spirit into the wilderness to be tempted by the devil. And he fasted forty days and forty nights, and afterward he was hungry.

Matthew 4:1–2

Easter is really the greatest feast of the Church year—greater even than Christmas! The reason for this is that by rising from the dead on Easter Jesus Christ fulfilled the work he had come to do, and he opened the gates of heaven to all mankind.

Lent

Just as we have Advent to prepare for Jesus' birth, so we have a special time called **Lent** to prepare for his Passion, death, and Resurrection. During Lent, we take time to think about how Jesus' great victory at Easter was only accomplished by suffering and death. We also remember that if we hope to share in Jesus Christ's Resurrection, we must also follow him by sharing his sufferings. We do this by trying always to do what God wants, even when it is hard, and by offering up our sufferings to Jesus. And since Jesus loved us so much that he suffered and died for us, we too should try to love him and each other with a generous love that is ready to make sacrifices. This is why during Lent we unite ourselves with Christ's suffer-

ings by prayer, by helping those in need, and by giving up some of our pleasures.

We know that Jesus was born to be King, but he was not the kind of king the people were expecting. "A king needs a crown and a fine robe!" the Roman soldiers must have laughed, for they made a crown out of thorns, pressed it onto his head, and wrapped him in a purple robe. Then they pretended to bow down to him. "Hail, King of the Jews!" they cried as they slapped his face and spat at him.

Jesus, who was a much greater king than David or Solomon, let them do these things because he knew that his was a different kind of Kingdom, one that only his suffering and death would bring about.

"Here is your King," cried Pontius Pilate to the people of Israel as he handed Jesus over to them to be crucified. As the people took Jesus off to carry his Cross to Calvary (the hill where they would kill him), Pilate had a sign put on the Cross. "THIS IS JESUS OF NAZARETH THE KING OF THE JEWS," it said in Hebrew (the language of the people of Israel). It was also written in Latin and Greek so that the Roman

149

"My people, what have I done to you? How have I offended you? Answer me!

"I led you out of Egypt from slavery to freedom, but you led your Savior to the
Cross.
"I opened the sea before you, but you opened my side with a spear.
"I bore you up with manna in the desert, but you struck me down and scourged
me.

"Holy is God! Holy and strong! Holy immortal one, have mercy on us!

"For you I struck down the kings of Canaan, but you struck my head with a reed.
"I gave you a royal scepter, but you gave me a crown of thorns.
"I raised you to the height of majesty, but you raised me high on a cross.

"My people, what have I done to you? How have I offended you? Answer me!"

The Divine Reproaches, Good Friday Liturgy

and Greek people living around Jerusalem could read it.

This made the chief priests furious. "You should not have written, 'The King of the Jews' ," they cried. "Write, 'This man *claimed* to be King of the Jews.' "

But Pilate said, "What I have written, I have written," and so the truthful sign was posted above the head of the true King who was dying for his people.

As the dead King hung on the Cross, a soldier came by to make sure that he was dead. With a spear, he pierced Jesus' side, and blood and water flowed out.

Jesus' friends took his body down from the Cross and lovingly placed it in a nearby tomb because the Sabbath was just about to start: it was Friday afternoon just before sundown. Later, after the Sabbath was over, they would come back and embalm his body.

Easter

Early Sunday morning while it was still dark, Jesus' good friend, Mary Magdalene, came to the tomb with spices to prepare his body for a proper Jewish funeral. But the stone had been rolled away from the entrance! So she ran to tell the Apostle Peter (who had been crying because he had denied knowing Jesus). She also told the Apostle John, whom Jesus had loved very much: "They have taken the Lord out of the tomb, and we do not know where they have put him."

Peter and John ran all the way to the tomb. They went inside. The cloth (called a shroud) in which the body of Jesus had been wrapped was lying there. Then Peter and John went home, but Mary Magdalene was grief-stricken, and she stood weeping outside the tomb. Then she stooped to look inside, and saw two men in

white sitting inside the tomb where Jesus' body had been. "Why are you weeping?" they asked.

"Because they have taken away my Lord and I do not know where they have put him," she said. Just then she turned away from the tomb and saw a man who she thought was the gardener. "Woman, why are you weeping? Who are you looking for?" he asked.

Mary thought that this man might have taken Jesus' body. "Please sir, if you have taken him away, tell me where you have put him, and I will take him away," she said.

In reply, the man just said, "Mary."

All at once Mary knew who it was. She turned and said in Hebrew, "Rabboni!" (which means Teacher).

Jesus said, "Do not hold on to me, for I have not yet ascended to the Father; but go to my brethren and say to them, 'I am ascending to my Father and your Father, to my God and your God.'"

Words to Know:

Lent

Words to Know

AARON: the brother of Moses. God made Aaron Moses' spokesman. Also, Aaron was the one who made the golden calf while Moses was up on Mount Sinai.

ABEL: Adam and Eve's second son. He was murdered by his brother, Cain.

ABRAHAM: the man who is remembered for his great faith in God. God made an agreement or covenant with Abraham: God would give him many descendants and take care of Abraham and his descendants if they believed and obeyed him. And Abraham always did this. His son was Isaac.

ABSOLUTION: the words said by the priest in the Sacrament of Penance which free us from our sins.

ACTUAL SIN: sin that we commit ourselves.

ADAM: the first man created by God.

ADVENT: the time of preparation before Christmas. We prepare for Jesus' birth and also for his coming at the end of the world. Advent means "coming."

ANGELS: pure spirits created by God.

ANOINTING: the act of putting oil on someone as a sign that God is giving his strength, power, or healing to him.

ANOINTING OF THE SICK: one of the seven sacraments. Through this sacrament, Jesus gives spiritual comfort and strength to dangerously sick people or people so old that they are in danger of death. It forgives sins and can also help people get well.

ARK: the boat built by Noah before the flood.

ARK OF THE COVENANT: (also called the Ark) the golden chest containing the Ten Commandments which was carried by the Hebrews during their desert journey to the Promised Land. King Solomon gave a permanent home to the Ark in the Temple of Jerusalem.

ASCENSION: Jesus' going up to heaven forty days after his Resurrection from the dead.

ASSUMPTION: the taking up of the body and soul of Mary into heaven.

BAPTISM: one of the seven sacraments. Through Baptism, Jesus cleanses a person of all sin. He is born again as a child of God and becomes a member of the Church.

BATHSHEBA: the wife of a soldier named Uriah. David fell in love with her and arranged to have Uriah killed in battle so that he could marry her. Solomon was their son.

BETHLEHEM: a city in the land of the tribe of Judah. Naomi, Jesse, and David were all from Bethlehem. Most importantly, Jesus was born in Bethlehem.

BISHOP: a leader of the Church who holds the place of an apostle. The bishops are the fathers and shepherds of our souls.

BLASPHEMY: using God's name disrespectfully, carelessly, or even hatefully. Irreverent thoughts, words, and actions for God and his Church are also blasphemy.

BOAZ: the relative of Naomi who married Ruth. Their child was Jesse, the father of David and the ancestor of Jesus.

CAIN: Adam and Eve's first son. Cain murdered his brother, Abel.

CANAAN: the son of Ham. His descendants went to live in the Promised Land and named it after him. God took the land away from the Canaanites and gave it to the people of Israel.

CHRIST: a Greek title meaning "anointed one," which was given to Jesus.

CITY OF DAVID: the city of Bethlehem. It was called the City of David because David was born there. David also named Jerusalem the City of David because he conquered it and lived there.

CONFESSION: the telling of one's sins to a priest in order to receive absolution.

CONFIRMATION: one of the seven sacraments. Through Confirmation Jesus strengthens with the Holy Spirit those who are already baptized, so that they may continue more firmly to be his followers in spreading and defending the faith by their words and actions.

CONSCIENCE: a judgment that an action is right or wrong based on God's laws.

CONSECRATED: someone or something that is specially blessed and set aside for God.

CONSECRATION: the most important part of the Mass. Jesus changes bread and wine into his Body and Blood through the words and actions of the priest.

COVENANT: a contract or agreement made between two persons. In the Old Testament, the important covenant was the agreement made between God and the people of Israel. But now, we have a New Covenant that will last forever. It was made between us and God by Jesus. God promises to free us from our sins and bring us to heaven. In return, we promise to give up our sins, be baptized, and follow Jesus and the Church.

COVET: to desire too strongly to possess things which do not belong to us.

DAVID: the second king of Israel, the son of Jesse of Bethlehem. He became famous when he killed Goliath, a gigantic Philistine soldier. He was a good king and people loved him. But he turned away from God to marry Bathsheba by arranging for her husband to be killed. When God punished him, David was very sorry and turned back to God again.

DELILAH: a woman who was bribed by the Philistine leaders to betray Samson, who loved her.

DESCENT INTO HELL: After his death on the Cross, Jesus went to the souls of all the dead, coming as the Savior to free the souls of the just who had died before his time.

DEVILS: those angels who refused to serve God and to do his will. They were created good by God but became evil by their own choice. They try to lead us away from God.

EDEN: the beautiful garden in which God put Adam and Eve when he created them.

ENVY: the sin of being resentful or saddened by another's success or possessions.

ESAU: the son of Isaac and Rebekah and the twin brother of Jacob. He sold his birthright to Jacob for a bowl of stew.

EUCHARIST: one of the seven sacraments. The Eucharist is the true Body and Blood of Jesus under the appearances of bread and wine. Because this Sacrament actually is Jesus himself, it is the most important and most blessed of the sacraments.

EVE: the first woman created by God. Eve was the wife of Adam.

FALSE WITNESS: lying about someone.

FAST: to do penance by skipping a meal or eating less food than usual.

FLATTERY: praising someone just so the person will do something for you; false praise.

FREE WILL: the ability to make a choice.

GENERAL JUDGMENT: the judgment of the entire human race at the end of the world.

GENTILES: people who are not Jews.

GOLDEN CALF: the idol that Aaron made for the Hebrews because they were tired of waiting for Moses to come down from Mount Sinai.

GOLIATH: a gigantic Philistine soldier, nine feet tall, whom David killed with a stone from his slingshot.

GOSPEL: one of the four accounts of the life, death, and Resurrection of Jesus in the Bible.

(Gospel comes from two words: "god" and "spell," meaning "good news.")

GOSSIP: the sin of worthless and useless talk, particularly about others.

GRACE: the free gift that God gives us by which he helps us to reach heaven.

HAM: one of the three sons of Noah. The Promised Land was named after his son, Canaan.

HEAVEN: eternal life and happiness with God.

HEBREWS: another name for the people of Israel.

HELL: eternal separation from God.

HOLY COMMUNION: primarily, the reception of the Body and Blood of Christ in the Eucharist, and, secondarily, our fellowship and union with Jesus and others in the Mystical Body of Christ.

HOLY DAY OF OBLIGATION: a special feast day, besides Sunday, when Catholics are required to participate at Mass and refrain from work.

HOLY ORDERS: one of the seven sacraments. In this sacrament, Jesus gives a man the grace and spiritual power to celebrate Mass, forgive sins, and to make others holy.

HOLY SPIRIT: God, the Third Person of the Holy Trinity.

HOLY TRINITY: the mystery of God as a unity of three Divine Persons in one God.

HOMILY: the explaining of the Word of God by the priest at Mass.

HONOR: to love, to respect, and to obey.

"I AM": God's name, which he told to Moses. It reminds us that God has no beginning and no end and that he is the source of all life. (The Hebrew word for "I am" is Yahweh.)

IDOL: any thing that is given the honor and worship that rightfully belong to God alone.

INFALLIBILITY: the Pope's freedom from error in teaching the whole Church in matters of faith and morals.

ISAAC: the only son of Abraham and Sarah. To test Abraham's faith, God ordered that he kill Isaac. Abraham was ready to obey at once but God stopped him. Isaac became the father of Jacob and Esau.

ISAIAH: one of the great prophets of the Old Testament. Isaiah foretold many things about the coming of Jesus.

ISRAEL: the new name God gave to Jacob. The Jewish people were named after him. They were called the people or the nation of Israel.

JACOB: the son of Isaac and Rebekah and the twin brother of Esau (see Israel).

JAPHETH: one of the three sons of Noah.

JERUSALEM: the city which David conquered shortly after he was made king. He brought the Ark of the Covenant to Jerusalem to a hill called Zion and eventually, the whole city of Jerusalem was often called Zion. King Solomon built the very first Jewish temple in Jerusalem. Jesus taught in Jerusalem and that is where he was crucified, died, and rose again. He also ascended into heaven just outside of Jerusalem.

JESSE: the father of King David and an ancestor of Jesus.

JEWS: those people who follow the traditions of the Old Testament and are waiting for the Messiah.

JOHN THE BAPTIST: the last and the greatest of the prophets before Jesus. John was the cousin of Jesus.

JORDAN RIVER: the main river of Israel. The children of Israel crossed it into the Promised Land, and Jesus was baptized in it by his cousin, John the Baptist.

JOSEPH: Jacob's favorite of his twelve sons. His envious brothers sold him as a slave to some merchants bound for Egypt. He became a great lord and in the end brought his brothers and his father to live in Egypt. Through him, the chosen people were saved from famine and came to live in Egypt.

JOSHUA: the man who took Moses' place to lead the Israelites into the Promised Land of

Canaan. Joshua led all the battles that the Jews first fought when they entered Canaan, including the battle of Jericho.

JUDAH: the fourth son of Jacob and Leah. His name was given to one of the twelve tribes. Jesse and his son, King David, were his descendants. Also, Jesus was a descendant of Judah. Judah is also the name given to one of the two kingdoms formed after Solomon's death.

JUDEA: the part of Israel where the Kingdom of Judah was. Bethlehem and Jerusalem were in it. Jesus spent much of his time in Judea.

LEAH: the eldest daughter of Laban, who tricked his nephew Jacob into marrying her. One of their children was Judah, who was the ancestor of Jesus.

LENT: a time of preparation before Easter when we follow Jesus more closely by giving special time to prayer, good deeds, and penance.

LITURGY OF THE EUCHARIST: the second and most solemn part of the Mass, where Jesus becomes present and the actual Sacrifice takes place. He also comes to his people in Holy Communion.

LITURGY OF THE WORD: the first part of the Mass in which God's word to us is read and then explained to us in the homily.

LIVING BREAD: another name for Jesus in the Eucharist. Jesus told his disciples that he would give them Living Bread, meaning himself.

MANNA: the name that the Hebrews gave to the bread which God sent them from heaven while they were wandering in the desert.

MARRIAGE: one of the seven sacraments. Through this sacrament, Jesus blesses the covenant of two baptized persons, as they become husband and wife. He gives them his grace to love and help one another and their children.

MARY: the Mother of Jesus and therefore the Mother of God.

MASS: The Mass is the very Sacrifice of the Cross taking place today on our altars; a memorial of Jesus' death and Resurrection; and a sacred meal in which we receive Jesus.

MESSIAH: the promised Savior of the people of Israel.

MIRACLE: an event that takes place outside of the ordinary working of nature's laws. A miracle is something that can only be accomplished by the power of God.

MORTAL SIN: a serious offense against the law of God, which destroys the life of grace in a person's soul. It requires full knowledge of the sin and consent.

MOSES: a very great prophet of the Old Testament. Moses was born in Egypt at a time when all the Hebrew baby boys were being killed. But God saved him so that he could lead the people of Israel out of Egypt. God gave him the Ten Commandments on Mount Sinai.

MYSTERY: a truth revealed by God which, even though it is not contrary to reason, our human minds will never be able to understand completely.

MYSTICAL BODY OF CHRIST: another name for the Church; the real but spiritual union of all the members of the Church: those on earth, in heaven, and in purgatory as one body with Jesus as the head.

NAOMI: the mother-in-law of Ruth.

NATHAN: the prophet who was sent by God to King David to tell him that God was displeased with his shameful conduct of planning Uriah's death.

NATURE: what a thing is.

NEW COVENANT: *see* Covenant.

NEW ISRAEL: a name we give to the Church and the new People of God.

NOAH: the Old Testament father whom God saved in the ark when he sent the great flood to wash the earth clean. His sons were Shem, Ham, and Japheth.

OATH: calling God to witness that what we say is true.

OCCASION OF SIN: any person, place, or thing that would tempt us to sin.

ORIGINAL SIN: the very first sin, which was committed by Adam and his wife, Eve, the parents of the human race. Because of original sin, mankind was separated from God and denied entrance into heaven. Because of original sin, we are all born without grace.

PAGAN: anyone who does not believe in the one, true God.

PARTICULAR JUDGMENT: the individual judgment by Jesus of each person after his death.

PASCHAL MEAL: another term for the Eucharist.

PASSOVER: the Jewish feast that God ordered to be celebrated every year so that the Israelites would remember how he rescued them from Egypt. It was called Passover because God "passed over" the people of Israel when he struck down the firstborn of the Egyptians. At Jesus' last Passover celebration before he died, he gave us the Eucharist.

PENANCE: one of the seven sacraments. Through this sacrament, Jesus forgives our sins and gives us grace to grow in holiness; penance also means prayers and good works done to make up for our sins.

PEOPLE OF GOD: another name for the Church; the people of the New Israel or the chosen people of the New Covenant.

PEOPLE OF ISRAEL: *see* Israel.

person: an individual being with intellect and will.

PETER: the leader of the apostles. Jesus made him the first Pope.

PHARAOH: a ruler in ancient Egypt.

PHARISEES: a Jewish group which existed around the time of Jesus. They grew so concerned about following the special Jewish laws very strictly that they forgot to love God and others.

PHILISTINES: the people who lived in Philistia. They were the constant enemy of the Hebrews for many years.

PLAGUE: a disastrous evil or affliction.

POPE: the chief leader and teacher of the Catholic Church; he takes the place of Jesus on earth.

PRAYER: the raising of the mind and heart to God; talking with God.

PROPHECY: God's message to his people. Sometimes prophecy is about the future.

PROPHET: a messenger chosen by God to speak to his people for him.

PSALMS: prayer-poems and hymns in the Old Testament inspired by God.

PURGATORY: the state after death which purifies souls and helps them to make up for sins committed while they were alive.

RACHEL: the second wife of Jacob. Jacob had to work a total of fourteen years to marry her, but he loved her very much. Their children were Joseph and Benjamin.

REBEKAH: the wife of Isaac. They had twin sons: Jacob and Esau.

RECONCILIATION: making peace; restoring friendship between two or more persons. In the Sacrament of Penance, the priest, in the Person of Jesus, forgives our sins and reconciles us to God.

REDEEM: to free someone from slavery by buying freedom for the person. Jesus redeemed us from slavery to sin and the devil by his death and Resurrection.

REDEEMER: a title for Jesus since he redeemed (freed) us from sin.

RESPECT: to think highly of and to show consideration for.

RESURRECTION: Jesus' rising from the dead under his own power as the Son of God.

RESURRECTION OF THE BODY: the raising by God of all bodies from the dead and the reuniting of them with their souls at the end of the world.

REVELATION: the truths of faith which God has made known to us through Scripture and Tradition.

REVERENCE: great respect.

RUTH: a pagan woman from Moab who married Naomi's relative, Boaz. They had a son, Jesse, whose son was King David, and Jesus was his descendant.

SABBATH: the day dedicated to God by prayer, rest, and worship; it is celebrated on Saturday by the Jews and on Sunday by Christians.

SACRAMENT: a sign given by Jesus that gives us grace. Jesus gave us seven sacraments through his Church.

SACRED: holy or divine.

SACRIFICE: the offering up to God of something that is dear to us.

SAMSON: a hero from the tribe of Dan. His great strength, which was associated with his long hair, was the undoing of many Philistines.

SAMUEL: the son of Hannah. He was a very holy prophet.

SARAH: the wife of Abraham.

SAUL: the first king of Israel. He was a good king at first but then he turned away from God.

SCANDAL: bad example which would lead others to sin.

SECOND ADAM: a name given to Jesus to show that as sin came into the world from the first Adam's disobedience, sin was conquered by the second Adam's obedience.

SECOND EVE: a name given to Mary to show that, as Eve helped Adam to sin, Mary was invited by Jesus to help him conquer sin.

SETH: Adam and Eve's third son, born after Abel's death.

SHEM: one of the three sons of Noah. The chosen people were descendants of Shem. Jesus was a descendant of Shem.

SIN: an offense against God's laws done on purpose by thoughts, words, actions, or omissions.

SIN OF OMISSION: not to do something that we should have done.

SINAI: a mountain near the Red Sea where God gave Moses the Ten Commandments.

SOLOMON: the third king of Israel, son of David and Bathsheba. He built the first permanent building for the Jews to worship God—the temple in Jerusalem. He is known for his great wisdom.

SOUL: the spiritual part of a person. It is individual and immortal.

TABERNACLE: a tent that represented God's presence with his chosen people. For us the tabernacle is also a holy place where God dwells. It is a container or box made out of fine materials where Jesus in the Blessed Sacrament is kept.

TEMPLE: the center in Jerusalem where the Jews worshipped God. Jesus spent time in the Temple, even as a little boy. A temple is also any place where God lives in a special way. Our bodies are temples of the Holy Spirit.

TEN COMMANDMENTS: the ten laws that God gave to the Jews and to us through Moses on Mount Sinai.

TOWER OF BABEL: a big tower built by proud people who thought that they could do things by themselves without God's help. God confused their language and so they had to abandon their tower.

TREE OF LIFE: a tree in the middle of the garden of Eden. Anyone who ate its fruit would live forever.

TREE OF THE KNOWLEDGE OF GOOD AND EVIL: a tree in the middle of the garden of Eden. To test their love, God forbade Adam and Eve to eat the fruit of this tree.

TRIBE: the families and descendants of one of Jacob's (Israel's) twelve sons. All of the chosen people became divided into tribes or families. Each received part of the Promised Land to live on, except for the tribe of Levi, the tribe of priests, who didn't need any land.

TRUTH: when what we say is the way things really are.

VENIAL SIN: a small sin. Venial sin weakens our friendship with God.

VICTIM: a living being offered in sacrifice to God.

VOW: a solemn promise made to God.

WITNESS: someone who can give testimony about someone else. In Christian vocabulary a witness is someone who gives testimony about Jesus to others. We witness to Jesus by good example, holy lives, or even by martyrdom.

YAHWEH: God's name which he revealed to Moses. In Hebrew, it means "I AM."

Prayers

THE SIGN OF THE CROSS

In the name of the Father, and of the Son, and of the Holy Spirit. *Amen.*

OUR FATHER

Our Father who art in heaven, hallowed be thy name. Thy kingdom come. Thy will be done on earth, as it is in heaven. Give us this day our daily bread, and forgive us our trespasses, as we forgive those who trespass against us, and lead us not into temptation, but deliver us from evil. *Amen.*

HAIL MARY

Hail Mary, full of grace, the Lord is with thee. Blessed art thou among women, and blessed is the fruit of thy womb, Jesus.

Holy Mary, Mother of God, pray for us sinners now and at the hour of our death. *Amen.*

GLORY BE

Glory be to the Father, and to the Son, and to the Holy Spirit. As it was in the beginning, is now, and ever shall be, world without end. *Amen.*

MORNING OFFERING

O Jesus, through the Immaculate Heart of Mary I offer thee my prayers, works, joys, and sufferings of this day in union with the Holy Sacrifice of the Mass throughout the world.

I offer them for all the intentions of thy Sacred Heart: the salvation of souls, reparation for sin, the reunion of all Christians.

I offer them for the intentions of our Bishops and of all Apostles of Prayer, and in particular for those recommended by our Holy Father this month. *Amen.*

THE APOSTLES' CREED

I believe in God,
   the Father Almighty,
   creator of heaven and earth.
I believe in Jesus Christ,
   his only Son, our Lord.
He was conceived by the power of the
   Holy Spirit
   and born of the Virgin Mary.
He suffered under Pontius Pilate,
   was crucified, died, and was buried.
   He descended into hell.
On the third day he rose again.
He ascended into heaven
   and is seated at the right
   hand of the Father.
   He will come again to judge
   the living and the dead.
I believe in the Holy Spirit,
   the holy catholic Church,
   the communion of saints,
   the forgiveness of sins,
   the resurrection of the body,
   and the life everlasting.
            Amen.

ACT OF FAITH

O my God, I firmly believe that thou art one God in three Divine Persons: Father, Son, and Holy Spirit. I believe that thy Divine Son became man and died for our sins, and that he will come to judge the living and the dead. I believe these and all the truths that the Holy Catholic Church teaches, because thou hast revealed them, who can neither deceive nor be deceived. *Amen.*

ACT OF HOPE

O my God, relying on thy infinite goodness and promises, I hope to obtain pardon of my sins, the help of thy grace, and life everlasting, through the merits of Jesus Christ, my Lord and Redeemer. *Amen.*

ACT OF LOVE

O my God, I love thee above all things, with my whole heart and soul, because thou art all good and worthy of all my love. I love my neighbor as myself for the love of thee. I forgive all who have injured me and ask pardon of all whom I have injured. *Amen.*

ACT OF CONTRITION

O my God, I am heartily sorry for having offended thee. I detest all my sins because of thy just punishments, but most of all because they offend thee, my God, who art all good and deserving of all my love. I firmly resolve, with the help of thy grace, to confess my sins, to do penance, and to amend my life. *Amen.*

THE ANGELUS

V. The angel of the Lord declared unto Mary.
R. And she conceived of the Holy Spirit.

Hail Mary. . . .

V. Behold the handmaid of the Lord.
R. Be it done to me according to thy word.

Hail Mary. . . .

V. And the Word was made flesh.
R. And dwelt among us.

Hail Mary. . . .

V. Pray for us, O holy Mother of God.
R. That we may be made worthy of the promises of Christ.

Let us pray. Pour forth, we beseech thee, O Lord, thy grace into our hearts, that we, to whom the Incarnation of Christ thy Son was made known by the message of an angel, may by his Passion and Cross be brought to the glory of his Resurrection. Through the same Christ Our Lord. *Amen.*

MYSTERIES OF THE ROSARY

The Joyful Mysteries

1. The Annunciation.
2. The Visitation.
3. The Nativity.
4. The Presentation.
5. The Finding in the Temple.

The Sorrowful Mysteries

1. The Agony in the Garden.
2. The Scourging at the Pillar.
3. The Crowning with Thorns.
4. The Carrying of the Cross.
5. The Crucifixion.

The Glorious Mysteries

1. The Resurrection.
2. The Ascension.
3. The Descent of the Holy Spirit.
4. The Assumption.
5. The Coronation.

LITANY OF LORETO

Lord, have mercy on us.
Christ, have mercy on us.
Lord, have mercy on us.
Christ, hear us.
Christ, graciously hear us.
God the Father of heaven,
have mercy on us.
God the Son, Redeemer of the world,
have mercy on us.
God the Holy Spirit,
have mercy on us.

Holy Trinity, One God,
have mercy on us.

Holy Mary, *pray for us.**
Holy Mother of God,
Holy Virgin of virgins,
Mother of Christ,
Mother of divine grace,
Mother most pure,
Mother most chaste,
Mother inviolate,
Mother undefiled,
Mother most amiable,
Mother most admirable,
Mother of good counsel,
Mother of the Church,
Mother of our Creator,
Mother of our Savior,
Virgin most prudent,
Virgin most venerable,
Virgin most renowned,
Virgin most powerful,
Virgin most merciful,
Virgin most faithful,
Mirror of justice,
Seat of wisdom,
Cause of our joy,
Spiritual vessel,
Vessel of honor,
Singular vessel of devotion,
Mystical rose,
Tower of David,
Tower of ivory,
House of gold,
Ark of the covenant,
Gate of Heaven,
Morning star,
Health of the sick,
Refuge of sinners,
Comforter of the afflicted,
Help of Christians,
Queen of Angels,
Queen of Patriarchs,
Queen of Prophets,

Queen of Apostles,
Queen of Martyrs,
Queen of Confessors,
Queen of Virgins,
Queen of all Saints,
Queen conceived without original sin,
Queen assumed into heaven,
Queen of the most holy Rosary,
Queen of peace,

Lamb of God, who take away the sins of the world, *spare us, O Lord.*
Lamb of God, who take away the sins of the world, *graciously hear us, O Lord.*
Lamb of God, who take away the sins of the world, *have mercy on us.*

Pray for us, O holy Mother of God.
That we may be made worthy of the promises of Christ.

Let us pray: Grant, we beseech Thee, O Lord God, unto us Thy servants, that we may rejoice in continual health of mind and body; and, by the glorious intercession of blessed Mary ever Virgin, may be delivered from present sadness, and enter into the joy of Thine eternal gladness. Through Christ our Lord. *Amen.*

THE STATIONS OF THE CROSS

1. Jesus is condemned to death.
2. Jesus carries his Cross.
3. Jesus falls the first time.
4. Jesus meets his Mother.
5. Jesus is helped by Simon of Cyrene.
6. Veronica wipes the face of Jesus.
7. Jesus falls a second time.
8. Jesus speaks to the women.
9. Jesus falls a third time.
10. Jesus is stripped of his clothes.
11. Jesus is nailed to the Cross.
12. Jesus dies on the Cross.
13. Jesus is taken down from the Cross.
14. Jesus is placed in the tomb.

*Pray for us is repeated after each invocation.

PRAYER FOR THE POPE

Father of Providence, look with love on *N.* our Pope, your appointed successor to St. Peter on whom you built your Church. May he be the visible center and foundation of our unity in faith and love. Grant this through Our Lord Jesus Christ, your Son, who lives and reigns with you and the Holy Spirit, one God, for ever and ever. *Amen.*

PRAYER FOR A BISHOP

Lord our God, you have chosen your servant *N.* to be a shepherd of your flock in the tradition of the apostles. Give him a spirit of courage and right judgment, a spirit of knowledge and love. By governing with fidelity those entrusted to his care may he build your Church as a sign of salvation for the world. We ask this through Our Lord Jesus Christ, your Son, who lives and reigns with you and the Holy Spirit, one God, for ever and ever. *Amen.*

PRAYER FOR VOCATIONS
by POPE JOHN PAUL II

O Jesus, our Good Shepherd, bless all our parishes with numerous priests, deacons, men and women in religious life, consecrated laity and missionaries, according to the needs of the entire world, which you love and wish to save.

We especially entrust our community to you; grant us the spirit of the first Christians, so that we may be a cenacle of prayer, in loving acceptance of the Holy Spirit and his gifts.

Assist our pastors and all who live a consecrated life. Guide the steps of those who have responded generously to your call and are preparing to receive holy orders or to profess the evangelical counsels.

Look with love on so many well-disposed young people and call them to follow you. Help them to understand that in you alone can they attain to complete fulfillment.

To this end we call on the powerful intercession of Mary, Mother and Model of all vocations. We beseech you to sustain our faith with the certainty that the Father will grant what you have commanded us to ask. *Amen.*

PRAYER FOR UNITY OF THE CHURCH

Almighty and merciful God, you willed that the different nations should become one people through your Son. Grant in your kindness that those who glory in being known as Christians may put aside their differences and become one in truth and charity, and that all men, enlightened by the true faith, may be united in fraternal communion in the one Church. Through Christ Our Lord. *Amen.*

MEMORARE

Remember, O most gracious Virgin Mary, that never was it known that anyone who fled to thy protection, implored thy help, or sought thy intercession, was left unaided. Inspired with this confidence, I fly unto thee, O Virgin of Virgins, my Mother: to thee do I come, before thee I stand, sinful and sorrowful. O Mother of the Word Incarnate, despise not my petitions, but in thy mercy hear and answer me. *Amen.*

PRAYER TO ST. MICHAEL

St. Michael, the Archangel, defend us in battle. Be our protection against the wickedness and snares of the devil. May God rebuke him, we humbly pray, and do thou, O prince of the heavenly hosts, by the power of God, thrust into hell Satan and the other evil spirits who prowl about the world seeking the ruin of souls. *Amen.*

EXAMINATION OF CONSCIENCE

How have I acted toward God? Do I think of God and speak to Him by praying to Him each day?

Do I speak of God with reverence?

Do I go to Mass on Sunday?

Do I do all I can to make Sunday a day of rest and joy for my family?

Do I participate in Mass, or do I tease or distract others by laughing, talking, or playing?

Do I pay attention to my parents, priests, and teachers when they talk to me about God?

How have I acted toward others?

Do I obey my parents and teachers quickly and cheerfully, or must I be reminded many times?

Do I tell my parents or those in authority over me that I am sorry and ask them to forgive me when I have not minded them?

Do I obey the rules of my home and school?

Do I help my brothers, sisters, and classmates when they need my help?

Am I kind to everyone?

Did I hit, kick, or in any way hurt others on purpose?

Am I willing to play with everyone?

Did I make fun or say mean things to anyone?

Do I do all my classwork and my chores at home well?

Do I take care of my health by eating the right food, etc.?

Do I think or do bad things or say bad words?

Do I tell the truth?

Do I say things about other people that are not true?

Did I cheat in class or in a game?

Did I steal or keep things that are not mine?

Am I willing to share my things with others?

Do I return things that I have borrowed?

THE PRAYER OF FATIMA

O my Jesus, forgive us our sins, save us from the fires of hell, and lead all souls into heaven, especially those in most need of thy mercy. *Amen*.

SPIRITUAL COMMUNION

My Jesus, as I cannot receive thee now in the Most Holy Blessed Sacrament, I ask thee to come into my heart, and make it like thy heart. *Amen*.

PRAYER TO MY GUARDIAN ANGEL

Angel of God, my guardian dear, To whom God's love commits me here, Ever this day be at my side, To light and guard, to rule and guide. *Amen*.

Art Credits